"Packed with insights and practical tools for moms about to send their teens into the real world. Whether our chicks are still in the nest or have already flown, Barbara and Susan's message will prepare and encourage every one of us. Several of my friends are rapidly approaching this time in their life, and they are fighting over this book!"

Shaunti Feldhahn, bestselling author
of *For Women Only* and *For Parents Only*

"These two friends give me clarity as I navigate the unfamiliar waters of being an empty nester. Their book is packed full of wisdom and encouragement about what it means to be a woman, a wife, a parent, a daughter, a friend, and most importantly, a kingdom builder!"

Rebecca Pippert, founder of Salt Shaker Ministries
and bestselling author

"This is the book I've been waiting for! Susan and Barbara offer encouragement and wisdom for adjusting to and flourishing in the empty nest. I plan to go through this book chapter by chapter with my friends."

Joy Downs, co-author of *Fight Fair* and *The Seven Conflicts*

"With my fourth child enrolled in a university a thousand miles away, I devoured *Barbara and Susan's Guide to the Empty Nest*! I especially appreciated the emphasis on taking time to reflect on my life story and then gearing up to embrace my future with both purpose and passion. We baby boomers always wanted to change the world; the good news is that we still can—as older, wiser, focused women of God."

Lucinda Secrest McDowell, speaker and author
of *Role of a Lifetime: Your Part in God's Story*

"The nest is no longer empty. Barbara and Susan have filled it up with opportunity, comfort, celebration, and friends."

Darcy Kimmel, co-author of several books on parenting,
grandparenting, and family relationships

"Six months after my children left for college, I was overwhelmed by a feeling of emptiness. Then I read this book. It gave me a profound sense of connection to other women in this transition. I felt recharged with a new excitement about the empty nest!"

Molly Shafferman says she is a "regular mom, no one famous"

"As a mother I felt lost and empty when the last of our four children left for college. And I didn't know where to find the answers. As Barbara and Susan candidly discuss this journey, you will laugh, get a little teary, and in the end, be encouraged."

Karen Loritts, conference speaker and co-author
of *Building Character in Your Children*

"Barbara and Susan give an honest look at the challenging transition that comes after years of child-rearing. They show that after a time of loss and loneliness, we can reinvent ourselves—creating a second season of life full of adventure and purpose. Bravo!"

Brenda M. Hunter, PhD, psychologist and author
of *In the Company of Women* and *Staying Alive*

"With true stories filled with practical how-to and Scriptures of encouragement these ladies have found the secrets to helping us through those dreaded years. Mothers, this is a must-read."

Thelma Wells, Women of Faith conference speaker
and bestselling author of *God Is Not Through With Me Yet*

# BARBARA AND SUSAN'S Guide TO THE Empty Nest

## Other Books From Barbara Rainey

*Letters to My Daughters: The Art of Being a Wife*

*Thanksgiving: A Time to Remember*

*When Christmas Came*

Growing Together Series (read-aloud stories for families)

## Other Books From Susan Yates

*And Then I Had Kids: Encouragement
for Mothers of Young Children*

*Character Matters: Raising Kids With Values That Last*

*One Devotional: One Word, One Verse,
One Thought for One Hundred Days*

*Risky Faith: Becoming Brave Enough to Trust
the God Who Is Bigger Than Your World*

REVISED AND UPDATED

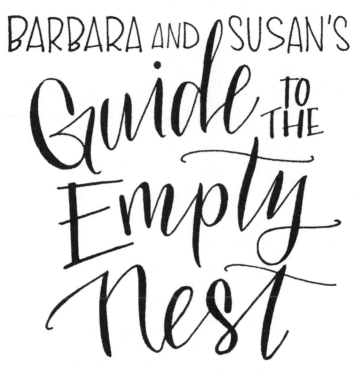

# BARBARA AND SUSAN'S Guide TO THE Empty Nest

Discovering New Purpose, Passion,
and Your Next Great Adventure

## BARBARA RAINEY AND SUSAN YATES

BETHANYHOUSE
a division of Baker Publishing Group
Minneapolis, Minnesota

Published by Bethany House Publishers
11400 Hampshire Avenue South
Bloomington, Minnesota 55438
www.bethanyhouse.com

Bethany House Publishers is a division of
Baker Publishing Group, Grand Rapids, Michigan

Printed in the United States of America

Previously published by FamilyLife Publishing

Library of Congress Cataloging-in-Publication Data
Names: Rainey, Barbara, author. | Yates, Susan Alexander, author.
Title: Barbara and Susan's guide to the empty nest : discovering new purpose, passion,
    and your next great adventure / Barbara Rainey and Susan Yates.
Other titles: Barbara & Susan's guide to the empty nest
Description: Revised and Updated Edition. | Bloomington, Minnesota : Bethany House,
    [2017] | Revised edition of the authors' Barbara & Susan's guide to the empty nest,
    2008. | Includes bibliographical references.
Identifiers: LCCN 2016043583 | ISBN 9780764219191 (trade paper : alk. paper)
Subjects: LCSH: Motherhood. | Empty nesters. | Parent and child.
Classification: LCC HQ759 .R255 2017 | DDC 306.874/3—dc23
LC record available at https://lccn.loc.gov/2016043583

The names of certain individuals have been changed in order to protect their privacy.

Cover design by Brand Navigation
Cover hand-lettering by Corey Powell, Rogers, Arkansas

Authors are represented by Wolgemuth and Associates

17  18  19  20  21  22  23      7  6  5  4  3  2  1

To the ten women who have prayed
faithfully for this project.

Judy Burrows, Kim Doerr, Wendy Habicht,
Elizabeth Law, Sue Mary, Tracee Persiko,
Barbara Riordan, Amy Rogers,
Debbie Sweek, and Nook Tuttle

We are so thankful for you, for your
friendship, and for your willingness to serve
us in what God has called us to do.

Your prayers have made all the difference!

# Contents

# Acknowledgments

We are both very grateful for so many people who have encouraged us along the way.

Our husbands, Dennis and John, have once again put up with empty refrigerators and no plans for dinner and loved us in spite of it!

The Rainey kids and Yates kids and their wonderful spouses have cheered for us and generously let us tell ridiculous and poignant stories on them.

The women to whom we have dedicated this book have prayed faithfully for us throughout this entire project. And other dear friends have once again supported each of us. Thank you, Molly Shafferman, Joy Downs, Mary Jenson, Judy Thomsen, Fran Cade, Ann Holladay, Julia Mitchell, Elaine Metcalf, Esther Powell, Karen Loritts, Merry Boehi, and Jackie Johnson.

We appreciate Susan's brother, Syd Alexander, for his legal advice in the chapter on caring for our parents and in-laws. Our "party friends," Sue Henry, Sally Rogers, and Jennie Lou Amy, have given us creative ideas for celebrating this season.

Thanks again to Tim Grissom, our first editor, coach, and friend. He not only made sure we produced an excellent book, but he also prayed for us in the process.

We appreciate the work of the whole Wolgemuth team, who guided us in this process. Thanks, Robert, Eric, and Andrew. And also to the Bethany House team, who have been so wonderful to work with: Andy McGuire, Natasha Sperling, and the entire design team. You have exceeded our expectations.

And to each one of the women who has let us share her story, we will always be grateful. In some cases we've changed her name for privacy, but each story is true. And we are thankful for you, our reader. You make our joy complete (1 John 1:4). We hope that as you join us in this adventure, you will discover new friends and a new purpose for this special season in life.

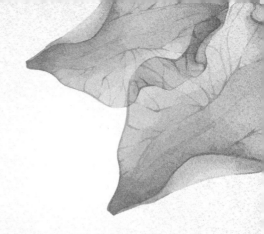

# PART ONE

## We're in This Together

# Chapter 1

## Who in the World Are Barbara and Susan?

A wise parent humors the desire for independent action, so as to become the friend and advisor when [her]
absolute rule shall cease.

Elizabeth Gaskell

So who are Barbara and Susan? Good question. If either of us
had pulled a book off the shelf and seen the names of authors
we didn't recognize, we'd wonder: *Who are these women? Why are
they writing this book? What do they have to offer me?*

When we first wrote this book several years ago, we were rela-
tively new to the season of the empty nest. Now that we are further
along in this season we are surprised at how relevant these concepts
are to women at every stage of the empty nest. Of all the seasons in
life, this one seems to have the most ebbs and flows!

In this revised and updated edition, we have added some new
stories and new lessons learned. As you'll discover in the pages that

follow, the empty nest is an evolving journey that still requires faith just as our years of parenting did.

Our bios in the back of the book don't tell you much about the real person, so right at the start we thought we'd tell you a little more about ourselves.

## Getting to Know Barbara

I clearly remember thinking that my mother was old the year she turned thirty-two. We were returning from an afternoon at the Warren Dunes State Park on the southern shores of Lake Michigan, and she had been pulled over by a policeman. For some reason she couldn't remember her age when the trooper asked. As an eight-year-old, I was amazed that she had forgotten and promptly helped by answering the question for her.

*She must have forgotten because she's old,* I thought. Never mind that she had three kids and visiting relatives in the car and was probably embarrassed and flustered. Somehow in that all-too-hasty assessment of my mother's age, I decided I would never grow old like my mom.

What on earth was I thinking? I'm way past thirty-two now; childhood and youth are a distant memory. I had six kids in ten years, did homeschooling and public schooling, and sent them off to college. I've orchestrated and helped with five weddings, survived a prodigal's years of rebellion, and started welcoming grandkids into the expanding Rainey clan. I'm still adjusting to my status as an "older" (not old, mind you) woman whose kids are grown.

My emotions, however, are more like those of my teen years—all over the place. I bounce between excitement and fear about the future. I've wondered what I'm good at, and I've pondered what choices I should make with my time. I look in the mirror and see the effects of aging that I was sure would never show up on my face and body. Some days I feel old and sad and tired, but most days I still feel as energetic and enthusiastic as I did in my twenties or thirties.

I remember my precious grandmother once telling me that sometimes when she walked by a store window and caught her reflection in the glass, she would do a double take, not recognizing the old woman in the window as herself. She told me she felt as young inside as she did at thirty. She was then in her early seventies, with beautiful silver hair and a wonderful heart of love. But to me she was old, nearly fifty years my senior, and I couldn't understand how she could feel anything other than old.

Now I understand. I'm discovering that this season of life is complicated and confusing, and there is no guidebook for walking this road. And I'm also seeing that this empty-nest journey is not a short, easy, or well-mapped hike. But I have concluded, for now anyway, that the cause behind my emotional wavering is a transitioning self-identity. At the core of this is the realization that I'm not needed as I once was.

Recently, I journaled these thoughts to try to make sense of what I was feeling:

> Before I married, I was looking for love. I daydreamed of being chosen, of becoming a bride, of being the most important person in his life . . . loved for a lifetime.
>
> Then, two years after the wedding, I discovered something new. Our first child, Ashley, was born, and I was instantly needed in a way I'd never been needed before. Yes, my husband had needed me before this child came into my life and he still does, but this baby and all the other children that followed needed me for their very survival. And that dependency changed my life.
>
> A mysterious change took place in me when I became a mother. Though the change was gradual, its roots grew down deep into my soul. Being a mother defined my life daily. It forced me out of bed early each day for thirty years. Caring for these little people consumed my thoughts. Guiding them, directing them, training them, disciplining them, praying constantly for them. I wanted to do it well. It gave my life purpose. It became my identity. "Mother" was who I was, and I considered it an honor.
>
> Though I had other interests that were often frustrated in their fulfillment, and though many of my daily tasks were often mundane

and aggravating, still the task of mothering was my life's purpose, my *raison d'être*. Long after my children were physically able to care for themselves, I knew they still needed me for comfort and love and direction and support.

And I discovered that I needed them. I had become attached to my role. I liked being important in their lives. It was deeply gratifying that when they got hurt, they always wanted me and no one else. No one could comfort them the way I could. Not even their dad. It felt good.

When Ashley left for college, I saw the end in sight. It was ten years away, but visible on the horizon. Knowing that the end of such a grand journey was nearing, I determined to invest in the experience all the more. In the last five or six years, I spent more time at the school volunteering than I ever had before. I drove the carpool to more games and events. I wanted to be where my teens were. I wanted to know their friends, their teachers, their world, because for so long they had been mine.

And now, now that the kids are gone, I wonder: Am I needed anymore? By anyone? Does anyone *really* need me?


## Getting to Know Susan

When we had five kids—including a set of twins—in seven years, I was overwhelmed. Those early years are now blurred memories of sleep deprivation, feelings of inadequacy, and amazement at the intensity of my love for each child.

And when those five became teenagers, the stakes seemed higher. How do I set limits yet let go? How do I prepare them to leave home? Would they be ready? Would I?

No matter how much I wanted to, I couldn't stop time. College applications were sent; acceptances and rejections came back, bringing tears of joy and outright despair. The applause of graduation became the trepidation of orientation. And then the good-byes came. Mixed emotions—stiff upper lips, joyous anticipation, free-flowing tears. There was simply no way to predict how each of us would react.

My twenty-one-inch newborn son who needed me every waking moment was now six-foot-two and pushing for independence.

Those two little twins fearfully climbing onto the bus for their first day of school were now stepping into wedding dresses to walk down the aisle.

And it all seemed to have gone by so fast. Too fast.

Because our kids were so close in age, we felt the intensity of the emptying nest for seven years as they all graduated from high school and left for college. In some ways I felt that I hardly had time to process what was happening; as soon as one left, there was another one preparing to leave. Still, with all the different breaks that college schedules brought, the kids were home a lot, usually bringing friends with them. So in those years the house didn't feel very empty.

Then life in the Yates household took another turn, when our oldest, Allison, got married right after graduating from college. John, our second oldest, was a junior in college. Chris was graduating from high school, and the twins, Susy and Libby, were sophomores in high school. We found ourselves dealing with the emotions of Allison and Will's wedding and Chris's leaving at the same time.

Over the next few years, our seasons continued to merge as all of our kids married young. In fact, we had four more weddings in three summers! Along the way I experienced a wide variety of emotions, but it wasn't until Susy moved her stuff out of our house the day after Libby's wedding that the permanence of the empty nest hit. I had a meltdown. This is my journal entry from that day:

Empty rooms.

I hate bare rooms. I really hate them when they are my daughters'. The pictures in Susy's room are down—that one of the twins hugging each other, the one showing crooked teeth and a silly grin surrounded by old-fashioned bangs, that first prom date depicting awkward posture, betraying nervousness mingled with excitement, glimpses of a lady about to burst forth from a child's body—a future and a hope.

Her closet used to be so full of things that you could hardly close the door. Hangers draped with her clothes, Libby's clothes, her brother's "cool" hand-me-down clothes. But now it's just a few empty hangers, and they are the "old timey" wire ones. She even took the good plastic ones with her!

Staring at emptiness, I see one old, discarded blue prom dress in the corner. It's way out of style. It hangs there lonely, out of place as if to say, "Where are all the others? I don't belong here all alone."

Just the way I feel.

My life was like that closet used to be. So crammed, so full, great diversity, comings and goings, opening and shutting doors, happy voices, phones ringing.

And now it's quiet. Too quiet.

I, like the old blue dress, feel deserted, lost, and out of place. Where are all the others? They belong here.

## Will You Join Us?

As you can see, we were two friends experiencing different phases of the empty nest. We both struggled with the awkward transition. We had many honest talks about what we were going through ourselves, and we talked to other women in various stages of the empty nest.

One of the main things we realized is that we need friends to walk through this season with us. Our husbands can't always appreciate the changes we face, and our mothers are from a different generation.

The empty-nest season is much like Jell-O, hard to grab hold of and constantly changing shape. There's no mold that we can pass on to others, no consistency. The empty nest affects us each differently, but there is comfort through friends who can reassure us that we are normal and who can remind us of a God who does have a plan.

We hope you will accept our invitation to join our friendship. We long for you to come alongside us as we grapple with questions like these:

- Has anyone else felt like I do now that my kids are gone?
- What now?

- Who am I?
- Who do I want to be?

We aren't psychologists or counselors. We're simply two friends who want to share what we've learned and what we're still learning. We want to give you hope for the future and challenge you to live out this season with new purpose and great adventure.

# Chapter 2

## Am I the Only One
## Who Feels This Way?

Friendship is born at that moment when one person says to another, "What! You too? I thought I was the only one."

C. S. Lewis, *The Four Loves*

It was a bright Saturday morning, perfect for the joyous occasion several of us were hosting. A sweet young friend was finally about to give birth after years of infertility, and we were celebrating by giving her a baby shower.

As I (Barbara) walked in the front door carrying my breakfast casserole, I was unprepared for the swirl of emotions I was about to experience. After helping to arrange the food table and welcome guests each time the doorbell rang, I joined a group of friends already engaged in lively conversation.

One friend was sharing about her daughter's first babysitting job and the funny story of how she dealt with a toddler's poopy diaper.

As the laughter quieted, another woman jumped in with a story about her son getting his driver's permit and how nervous she felt about it. Still another mother joined in with a "You won't believe this!" about her child's driving antics.

The adventures of motherhood was clearly the topic for the day. They were good stories, all, and I longed to share some of my own. But I couldn't. For the first time in over twenty-five years, I had nothing to contribute to the let-me-tell-you-what-my-child-is-doing conversation. Apart from listening to and laughing at the friendly exchanges of their present-tense mothering, it became clear that I was now past tense.

My emotions assaulted me as I listened—*You've been demoted, kicked out of the mothering club. You're on the outside now. You don't belong.* I grew painfully aware that this new season I had moved into felt a little like . . . death.

What made this so difficult to deal with was that it was so unexpected. My youngest had been in college almost a full year, and I thought I'd passed beyond all of this struggle months before.

Needing a break from the happy chatter, I retreated to the kitchen and started washing dishes. *At least I'll be doing something useful,* I thought. But wouldn't you know it, the conversation in the kitchen was more of the same! A different group, but the same topic.

The longer I listened, the more excluded I felt. I remember thinking, *I can't wait for this party to be over so I can leave and go home.*

### Feeling Like Freshmen

One of our friends observed, "Entering the empty-nest years is a lot like going to college." And she's right. Like college-bound teens, we look forward to the freedom ahead, perhaps planning some remodeling possibilities with empty bedrooms, much like freshman girls do with their dorm rooms. New college students sign up for classes that sound exciting during orientation, but they have no idea what it will really be like, and that makes them a bit nervous. They rationalize that others have gone before, so it can't be *that* hard. And who cares? College will be fun.

In a similar way, we might anticipate the freedom to try a new job or career, to reconnect with our husbands, to travel to new places, perhaps also to return to college and take a few classes. A bit of nervousness is always lurking in the back of our minds, but other women have made this journey, so it can't be *that* hard.

Just as many unexpected adjustments await our newly launched children, we empty-nest women also find ourselves with unanticipated adjustments to loneliness, fears, and feelings of rejection. Though we are older and wiser than college-bound teens, we are nonetheless destined to learn more about who we are and what we believe in the months and years ahead as we journey on this road called The Empty Nest.

## Where the End and the Beginning Collide

Author Anna Quindlen, in her book *Loud and Clear*, wrote about the emotions she faced with her own empty-nest experience:

> Tell me at your peril that the flight of my kids into successful adulthood is hugely liberating, that I will not believe how many hours are in the day, that my husband and I can see the world, that I can throw myself into my job. My world is in this house, and I already had a great job into which I'd thrown myself for two decades. No, not the writing job—the motherhood job. I was good at it, if I do say so myself, and because I was, I've now been demoted to part-time work. Soon I will attain emerita status. This stinks. . . .
>
> The empty nest is emptier than ever; after all, at its center was a role, a vocation, a nameless something so enormous that a good deal had to be sacrificed for it, whether sleep or self or money or ambition or peace of mind. . . .
>
> In the kitchen is a magnet that says "Mom is NOT my real name."
>
> It's not simply the loss of these particular people, living here day in, day out, the bickering, the inside jokes, the cereal bowls in the sink and the towels in the hamper—all right, on the floor. It was

who I was with them: the general to their battalion, the president to their cabinet. . . . Sometimes I go into their rooms and just stand, touching their books, looking out their windows.

She concludes her thought with a line that summarizes our conflict of identity: "Mom is my real name. It is, it is."[1]

Both of us feel again the pang of our own loss and grief just reading Anna Quindlen's words. We long to hang on to that identity we have known for so long, "the general to their battalion, the president to their cabinet." But we have to embrace the transition if we are to be healthy. Leaving the world of mothering is necessary for us and for our children. Moving on is the challenge.

There is a wonderfully descriptive word for the emotions of empty-nest women: *ambivalence*—experiencing two opposing feelings at the same time. Counselors use this term frequently to help clients understand that as humans we can and often do experience contradictory emotions: love and hate, anger and joy, grief and celebration. Ambivalence is felt most strongly with our closest relationships—parents, siblings, spouses, and children—and in situations that are part of the normal rhythm of family life: parenting, marital harmony (or dissonance), graduations, weddings, and deaths.

If the hundreds of women we've talked to are a reliable marker, and we think they are, it's clear that we are given to experiencing polar emotions in short cycles—sadness, hope, loneliness, expectancy, anxiety, peace, and back and forth and on and on. Are any of the following emotions yours right now?

- *Loneliness, rejection, and isolation* because you no longer belong to the motherhood club.
- *Joy, hope, excitement, and expectation* because you look forward to the future and new adventures.
- *Fear, anxiety, and uncertainty* because you don't know what is ahead for you and your husband.
- *Peace and tranquility* because you have finished well.

- *Failure, frustration, and hopelessness* because you have experienced great loss with one or more of your children or with your husband.
- *Personal insecurity and loss of confidence* because you have no idea what you are good at anymore.

The end of mothering and the beginning of the empty nest is like the meeting of the ocean with dry land. In some places the shoreline is cragged, wild, and perilous, while in other locations the ocean rolls gently onto a smooth, restful beach. The shorelines of our emotions are equally varied and as vulnerable to changing circumstances as is the coast to the tides and weather. But take courage. Someone once said, "The ship won't sink and the storm won't last forever."

## We're in This Thing Together

The invitation read,

*If you would like to join in a lively discussion
of the season of the empty nest, please come for
dessert at my home next Tuesday evening.*

I (Susan) had no idea who or how many would show up. I imagined there would be mainly women with seniors in high school, but I was in for a surprise. The twenty-three women who gathered at my home that evening ranged from a mother whose oldest was a sophomore in high school to a young widow whose kids were grown.

One mom whose daughter had just left for college blurted out through her tears, "I cry every day. After all these years, nobody needs me. I feel like I've been fired!"

An older mom surprised us by saying, "My daughter just turned forty, and this has been so hard on me. I feel like an empty nester all over again."

A younger mom whose eldest was sixteen shared that she was already anxious about the kids leaving. "What should I be doing now to get ready?" she wanted to know.

Another mom exclaimed, "I'm so glad to have an empty nest! Finally I have time for me!"

As I listened to the women share with amazing vulnerability, it became clear to me that there is no single circumstance that defines the empty nest. Unlike the seasons of parenting toddlers or teens, this season is ambiguous—it has no clear beginning. Often when you think you've come through it to a place of peace, it hits you all over again like it did for Barbara. So many unique factors play a part in determining when and how the emotions of the empty nest will affect you.

For Tracy, the empty nest began early. Leaving an attractive career, she had chosen to stay home to raise her precious only child. And now he was a junior looking at colleges and preparing to leave. Browsing through college brochures made her feel incredibly sad.

Sally's experience was different.

> I wasn't at all sad when we left our eldest at college. She was so excited and I was excited for her. I wasn't even sad when our son joined her at the same school two years later. But when our third left for school in a different state, I fell apart. He wasn't even our last child; we still had kids at home. But I think it took doing this three times to finally realize that a huge part of my life was changing. I had been too busy to really *feel* what was happening.

Later that evening as I put the dessert dishes away, I asked myself how I would describe the evening. One word came to mind—comforting. Even though the women present represented different stages in life, most experienced similar emotions. There's comfort in realizing that we are not alone.

### And the Waves Just Keep on Crashin'!

For many, the transition from full-time mother (even if we worked outside the home) to empty nester hits at about the same time in life

28

as other challenges. Being alert to these reefs and currents enables us to make the crossing with greater courage and calm.

Do you see any of the following converging on your life, and can you see how they might challenge and complicate your arrival at the empty nest?

**1. Your age.** If you're in your forties and feeling energetic, that works in your favor. If you're in your sixties and slowing down, you might need to give yourself a little extra grace . . . and hope that others will do the same.

**2. Menopause.** Full-blown menopause will keep you from sleeping at night, make simple decisions like what to wear seem gargantuan, and pull you into a game of hide-and-seek with your car keys and purse. (And those are the milder symptoms.) Perimenopause can bring just as much confusion and often lasts longer. I (Barbara) can see clearly through hindsight that during much of my forties I was experiencing perimenopause. I didn't understand then what was behind my random feelings of confusion, sadness, and fatigue. Now I know that menopause has a little sister named perimenopause that sometimes comes calling several years in advance.

**3. Your parents' health and needed care.** Those who are in the last years of raising their kids often have parents who are still alive but are failing in health and in need of care. We are called the "sandwich generation" with good reason. Dennis and I (Barbara) experienced that in full force as our last two children were teens and Dennis's mother was dying with Alzheimer's disease. It proved to be difficult and often impossible to visit her as often as we felt we should.

Being compassionate to the loss my husband was experiencing took me to one set of emotions, while keeping up with the pace of our teenagers and their lives required me to engage an entirely different set. These two completely different situations often caused me to feel that I was nearing emotional overload. Add perimenopause to the mix, and the atmosphere was sometimes electric!

**4. Your husband's expectations.** Some men haven't had the time to consider the approaching empty nest or what it will mean to you or to him. Others have thought about it and are anticipating a renewed relationship with their wives. Several women have said to us, "My husband can't wait to have me back." Dennis said that to me numerous times. He hoped that I would want to travel with him more when the kids left home, come to the office on a regular basis, and work in a cube next to him. And he expressed interest in my joining him in his recreational interests of hunting, fishing, and playing golf.

Do you know what your husband is thinking? Do his expectations sound overbearing to you, or does the realization that he hasn't thought about it disappoint you?

Take a breath. Think for a minute. His hopes are not illogical. When you married, your husband chose you for who you were as the woman he loved, the woman who eagerly joined him in his interests because you were in love. He didn't love you for the children you would bear or the kids you already had.

Many men feel that they shared us with the children for all those years. They feel that they sacrificed much of their time and relationship with us for the sake of the children, and now many are anticipating a return to the way things were.

When we look at the empty nest from a husband's perspective, it makes sense why they would feel this way. It may not be clear yet, but they will have adjustments, too. This isn't just a woman's issue.

**5. Number of children you raised.** The child-raising season lasted longer and cost more financially and emotionally if you parented many children. Mothers who raised two, three, or more children have a greater variety of experiences because of the unique personality of each child. And they have a more gradual transition into the empty nest than mothers who raise one child.

Etta, the mother of an only child, wrote to say, "A major difference for the parent of an only child is that once this child leaves home, there is no more opportunity to do it again, to apply lessons learned, to make up for what you felt was missing by changing what you've done with the other children. The end is abrupt and you have no second chance with another child."

**6. Level of involvement in your children's lives.** We have a theory that the greater your involvement in your children's lives as you raised them, the greater loss you feel when they leave home. That's not to say being an involved parent is a bad choice. Quite the opposite. But if you are at all the ball games, volunteer at school, make your house the center of activity, drive the carpool regularly, or homeschool your children through high school, your loss will seem greater. When the last child leaves home, all these activities stop. You can still go to the volleyball or football games if you want, but it won't be the same and you're likely to be asked, "What are *you* doing here?" You'll feel more of a loss if you identified closely with your child's world.

**7. How successful you feel with your children.** Did you finish well, and are they on a good path? Parenting can be messy and unpredictable; many of us cross the finish line with a child who has not chosen the path in life that we had hoped. Some children are outright rebellious, bringing parents one heartache after another. If we experience the kinds of losses associated with kids who reject our values—perhaps even dropping out of school or running away from home—we don't have much to rejoice in when the nest empties. When our dreams for our children die, or our hopes fade, we may limp painfully rather than walk easily into the next season of our lives.

**8. Your career.** Do you work or have a fulfilling interest outside of your home? Several women who have full- or part-time jobs have told us that their transition was not terribly difficult because they still had a reason to get up every day after the kids left. While they miss the children being there, they may not be as lonely as the moms who stayed in the home full-time. Still, they are not without adjustments. One working woman exclaimed, "Since our kids left, my husband and I don't know what to do with our free time in the evenings. We feel bored!"

**9. Your health.** Have you arrived at the empty nest in good health, or are you battling a physical ailment? The more issues that demand your attention, the more complicated your transition will be.

**10. Your financial needs.** Many women go back to work when their kids are in school. We all know that the bills during the high school and college years seem to multiply! In some situations you may encounter unexpected setbacks; for example, your husband gets laid off from work, and you learn again that what preys on your finances can threaten your marriage.

**11. Your personality.** Are you an optimist or a pessimist? Do you enjoy a new challenge or resist change? Are you a driven person or a relaxed, go-with-the-flow type? Who you are will determine much of your approach to this new season of life.

**12. Your husband's job—intensity, change, or possible retirement.** In marriage you are one with your spouse, and what happens to one affects the other. While you're trying to understand what's happening in your body and mind and in the use of your time, your husband's job is affecting who he is and how he is or is not responding to you. A man's career often escalates when he's in his forties and fifties, many times coinciding with the approaching empty nest. Is your husband's career on an upswing, bringing added pressure? Or is the opposite true? He's in a company that is cutting jobs, and he's worried that his might be next. Perhaps he is contemplating a vocational change or wanting to retire and move to a more rural setting, which would mean new relationships for you and lots of work. Perhaps he wants to do something radically different with his life. Is he experiencing a bit of a midlife crisis?

Don't let this list of potential challenges overwhelm you. Your personal list will likely be much shorter—not everyone's experience is the same. Still, there is a lot going on in your life in this new season, and you can find comfort in recognizing that you have many things in common with other women. You are not alone.

The two of us confidently believe that this empty-nest season can be our most exciting, productive season of life. We want to give you a shopping bag full of ideas, resources, and suggestions in the second half of the book. But first we want to look more at the common experiences we women face and give some practical solutions for this transition: What do we do with our loneliness?

Our disappointments? How might we need to adjust our marriage relationship? How do we relate to our adult kids? Can we discover a new vision for our lives? Is there more fun to look forward to?

Our prayer is that as the two of us honestly share our struggles and tackle our challenges, you will find comfort together with us and press on toward discovering the new purpose that has been prepared for us in this new season of life.

> The Lord gives strength to his people; the Lord blesses his people with peace.
>
> Psalm 29:11 NIV

## Take the Next Step

• • • • •

At the end of each remaining chapter, you will find questions to consider, resources that can assist you, and steps to take to help you process this transition in life. We hope you will use these in conversation with your husband and with other women. To be in community with others on this journey will benefit your marriage, your friendships, and your personal experience.

1. Start by sharing your own list of challenges with your husband for the purpose of greater understanding. This conversation will help him know what you are dealing with and how you are feeling. He can't be sympathetic if he has no idea what is swimming through your head and heart.

2. Take the same step with a friend. Find camaraderie over coffee. Or be really bold and invite a group of women over—like Susan did—and discover a great variety of experiences. You'll probably share a lot of laughs, too.

# Karen's Story

## Pulling Threads of Our Past Into Our Future

When her youngest daughter left for college, Karen hit a slump. She and Holly were unusually close, so she felt as though she was losing both a daughter and a friend.

It wasn't that Karen was unprepared; she'd been thinking about the empty nest as each of her four kids left home. And even though she was a hands-on mom, she'd also been heavily involved in the community; she had a life outside of her family. But Holly's departure released a sadness that Karen hadn't expected, so she turned to her friends.

Even though I didn't grow up with sisters—or a close relationship with my mother—God had given me older women who mentored me since junior high and a circle of friends whom I'd known for more than twenty-five years. The Lord had also placed several women in my life who had already experienced the empty nest. He used all of these to help me face the challenges.

Even though I felt embarrassed, I went to them and said, "You need to help me through this. Don't let me withdraw. Call me and ask me how I'm doing. Make sure I'm at Bible study and that I'm getting exercise. Help me stay involved. Pray for me to catch a fresh vision for my life."

These women let me be sad but didn't let me get stuck. They encouraged me to continue with the things I was already involved in, and they stayed in touch. They wouldn't let me hide, and they would gently remind me to take my eyes off myself. They prayed for me.

I needed these friends. I didn't want to phone Holly or the other children too often. That wasn't fair to them. They needed to move on, and they needed their mom to move on, too.

In contemplating my future, I considered my passions. I'd always loved teaching and discipling others, and I had been in on several ministry start-ups. I also had a background in the corporate world and in grant writing.

I knew God had made me a people person, and I wanted to make a difference in the lives of others.

I was already involved in a ministry called Wellspring Living,[2] which provides housing and hope for women coming out of substance, physical, and sexual abuse in the Atlanta area. I escalated my involvement in this outreach.

Another concern that tugged at Karen's heart was women prisoners. Through her work with the United Way and a national Christian foundation, Karen had been exposed to many needs and ways to finance ministries. She connected with an organization that provided a halfway home for women just being released from prison. With her background it was a natural fit for Karen to do some grant writing for this worthy cause.

Of course, taking on new challenges meant stepping back from others. Karen realized she had to be wise in both letting go and taking on. She said,

> A group of friends and I were discussing many needs in our city. After lots of talking, dreaming, and soul searching, we decided to start a foundation—the One Hundred Shares, Inc.—to support Christian ministries in the greater Atlanta area that care for those in need as well as proclaim the gospel. We asked one hundred women to pledge one thousand dollars a year for five years.[3]

Karen is always learning and always intentional in caring for others. Over the years she's invested herself in relationships with peers and with older women.

> What has been so clear to me in this transition is that we need friends with whom we can be honest. We need girlfriends—both younger and older—who will ask us hard questions and hold us accountable for our time with the Lord, for the use of our God-given gifts, and for our relationships with our husbands.
>
> I've also seen how God uses our natural talents and passions, as well as our past skills, in the new endeavors He has for us. He pulls threads from our past into our future. He never wastes anything.

# PART TWO

# Let's Get Honest

## Chapter 3

# What Do I Do With My Loneliness?

A friend is in prosperity a pleasure, a solace in adversity, in grief a comfort, in joy a merry companion, at all times another I.

John Lyly, *Euphues*

Tears streamed down Sarah's face as she began to describe how she was feeling. "Our last child has just left for college, and I find myself crying almost every day. For thirty years I've poured my life into my kids. Even though I started two of my own companies and was very successful, my kids were always my priority. Now nobody really needs me. I feel like I've been fired. I am so lonely."

Loneliness can catch us unawares. Georgie experienced it in the auto repair shop. As she was standing in line at the checkout counter, a song started playing over the speaker. It was one of her son's favorites. In fact, his band had played it, and just hearing it brought back memories of all the nights of band practice in their basement. To the astonishment of the clerk, Georgie burst into tears. Her son had only been gone two months, and her heart was still tender.

Nadine felt the loneliness most at the dinner table. Her husband and daughter used to joke around and mealtimes were full of laughter. Now, conversation between her and her husband seemed forced, even boring. The cloud of loneliness was thick. And it wasn't much fun to cook anymore.

Julia, a single parent, has raised her kids alone. Her daughter is a senior, and as they look at colleges, Julia wonders what the empty nest will be like for her.

> One thing I'm realizing is that being a single parent has some hidden blessings. I know what it's like to be alone; I've learned to be alone. It doesn't frighten me. I know I will experience loneliness in a fresh way when Liz leaves, but I am comfortable with being by myself. I've had to learn that. Feeling lonely because I miss my child is different from being miserable being alone. And I've learned that if I'm too lonely, it's my own fault. I need to reach out to someone else.

Loneliness, emptiness, a never-ending void—but it's not all bleak. There's also joy in finally having some time just for ourselves!

At some level each of us experiences loneliness during the empty nest. It's different for everyone. We can't always anticipate when or how it will hit us. Remember, it's like Jell-O—leaky, runny, and erratic! However, simply acknowledging loneliness and naming it brings a certain amount of relief.

## Contributing Factors to Loneliness

Although our experiences will vary, there are at least four factors contributing to our sense of loneliness.

### 1. Loss of Motivation

I (Susan) remember when I used to long for some free time so I could get things done, but the kids and their needs left little time for "other stuff."

40

Like all mothers, I became adept at multitasking. It was the only way to accomplish anything. I could interview another mom at a ball game for an article while watching the kids play. I could clean out kitchen cupboards while overseeing homework at the kitchen table. I was driven; I was motivated. Feeling that I was accomplishing several things at once gave me a lift. But then the kids left; when I cleaned the kitchen, it was just that. When I worked at my desk, it was just that. And I found that I didn't want to clean out the kitchen cupboards. It wasn't enough.

I also found it hard to do the creative things I liked to do—hanging pictures, putting together a photo album, redecorating. Why? Because my daughters weren't there to rave. I couldn't look forward to them walking in the door and saying, "Oh, Mom, that looks great!" My husband doesn't think to respond that way. Men rarely rave. It's just not the same.

Sometimes our motivation dwindles because there is no one there to appreciate or at least to recognize our efforts. It's lonely.

### 2. Loss of Confidence

If we have put our other careers on hold to be at home with kids, we may experience a bit of panic. *What am I going to do now? What can I do? The world seems to have flown past me. I've been out of the marketplace too long. How do I reengage?*

These questions are in the front of Pam's thinking. For nearly thirty-five years she's been a mom. Her six kids have been spread out age-wise, and she's chosen to homeschool the youngest ones. As she contemplates their leaving, she says, "I don't know who else I am besides a mom. I don't know what I'm interested in or even what I like. I feel that I'm already going through an identity crisis, and I still have one at home!"

When her second daughter left for college, Dawn was unprepared for the depression that hit. Even though she'd been involved in teaching at her children's schools, she'd done it merely to be near them. It wasn't really "her thing." In fact, she didn't like it all that much. Now she was sad, lonely, and a little angry with herself.

41

"Why didn't I find a career that I liked?" she wondered. She felt lost. "At fifty-two, what am I supposed to do? I don't even know how to begin to find a new career. I don't even know what I like or what I'm good at!"

Her confidence was shaken, and it was magnified by her loneliness.

### 3. Loss of a Clearly Defined Community

One of the most surprising things that many empty nesters experience is a loss of connection with other people. It's hard when many of your friends still have children at home and are talking about things you're no longer a part of. Weekends that were once filled with your child's athletic events and social engagements are now suddenly empty. The calendar is strangely void of adult camaraderie that used to take place around the common interests of teenagers.

Looking back, we realize that for most of our parenting life our friendships developed with the parents of our children's friends. When we were mothers of young children, we were desperate to be around other young moms in the same situation. They understood us. They knew how we felt. They were exhausted, too. There were MOPS[1] groups, study groups, and play dates. We could talk as our kids played. And then as we approached the teen years, we had friends with whom we could discuss the issues of curfews, movies, peer pressure, and setting limits. We had a natural bond. We sat at ball games together. We were all in the same boat.

Often in the teen years, we laid aside deep interaction with other adults. We were busy being available to our teens, being at home on weekends so they could have their friends over. In some ways we put our own social lives on hold in order to spend these last years with our kids.

And now we have time. But not all of our friends are empty nesters yet. And some have already launched into their next career. They aren't where we are. It's hard to identify someone in our season. There isn't a child alongside to give you a clue.

Without a friend to talk to, we are lonely.

### 4. Loss of Identity

SUSAN: The phone rang one morning shortly after the twins left for college. Our recorded greeting still said, "This is the Yates family. Leave us a message and we'll call you back."

It was Susy calling. Upon hearing the greeting she left a message: "Hey, Mom, it's weird to hear the answering machine still say 'Yates family' because it doesn't seem like it's much of a family anymore."

The very next message was from her twin, Libby.

"Hi, everyone," she said, "though it seems like the 'everyone' is shrinking!"

Fortunately my response was to burst out laughing. After all, we were still a family. We had just dispersed. But these comments did highlight the fact that our identity was changing.

It doesn't matter if we've sent our kids off with joy or sadness, felt relief when that difficult child left, hoped the prodigal wouldn't come home for a while, or wept when that child who was our dearest friend pulled out of the driveway. Our identity, to a large extent, had been defined by having kids at home. But it's no longer that way. It's a new season and we have to make adjustments.

### Adjusting to the Grand Adventure

Three adjustments will help ease the pain of loneliness and give you a fresh perspective on what can become a grand adventure:

### 1. Recognize the Season Principle

Over the years, both of us have found it helpful to recognize what we call the Season Principle. There's the season of being single, of being a newlywed, of raising young children, and of parenting teens. And the empty-nest season. Then for some comes the "bungee cord season," when the kids we thought had left bounce back to live at home again. And finally there are the golden years at the twilight of life. Seasons aren't purely biological; interspersed through life are seasons of loss, seasons of pain, seasons of stress, seasons of joy.

It's helpful to look at life in terms of seasons. Every season will have unique challenges and each season will have unique blessings. We all remember the challenges of the infant years: sleep deprivation and a lack of appreciation. It's a rare four-year-old who says, "Mommy, you are doing such a good job of raising me. Thank you!"

But those years also hold unique blessings. I (Susan) remember when Libby saw the ocean for the first time. As her little eyes grew wide with fright and amazement, she exclaimed, "Mommy, it's too full. You need to let some of it out!" Toddlers say funny things. It's a blessing unique to that season—teenagers don't often say funny things.

The teen years bring challenges—arguing, for one. Their arguments are so much better than ours, and they make us feel silly. It seems that the other parent is always more popular, more fun. And our feelings get hurt. But the teen years are full of blessings, too. We see hints that our children did learn some things along the way. They occasionally offer to help with the dishes or run an errand. In the later teen years, we notice two siblings who used to fight nonstop begin to actually like each other.

It's helpful to articulate the challenges and then choose to focus on the blessings of each distinct season. When we define the challenges and discuss them with others, we discover that we are normal! When we are intentional in looking for the blessings, we discover the joys that God has prepared for us. It's important to remember that no season lasts forever. We want to *really live* in each unique time and miss nothing.

So what about the season of the empty nest? We are already discovering some of the common challenges—that's one of the purposes of this book. But we don't want to remain stuck in the challenges. Instead, we want to focus on the benefits of this season. And most importantly, later in this book we will begin the process of discovering the next great adventure that awaits each one of us. Yet no matter what our current challenge is, the place to begin is with God.

### 2. Run to God

At different times every one of us will get stuck. We'll feel blue, we'll experience loneliness, we'll be anxious about the future. It isn't just being in the empty nest, it's being in transition. Moving from one season to another is uncomfortable and awkward. In fact, as much as we'd like to think *stability* is the norm in life, we actually spend more time in *transition*.

Where do we go in a time of transition? The book of Proverbs has a piece of advice for us: "The name of the Lord is a strong tower; the righteous runs into it and is safe" (Proverbs 18:10).

Our inclination can be to run to our husbands, our mothers, even friends. We might try to hold on to our children in an unhealthy way—unhealthy for them and for us. Or our tendency can be to wallow in our loneliness. While others can be helpful, ultimately it is God alone who will offer comfort and help us move forward.

Once, in the midst of a hard time, I (Susan) discovered a truth in the book of Hebrews that has radically changed how I run to God. Hebrews is a first-century letter that was written to the Jews who believed that Jesus Christ was the Messiah. In fact, much of the letter explains how Jesus fulfilled the role of the Messiah that they had been waiting for.

In this letter we learn that Jesus had to be made like us in all things in order to be able to make atonement for us. This means that He became our substitute, taking the punishment that, in fact, should be ours (see Hebrews 2:17).

We also learn that Jesus is able to sympathize with our weaknesses because He, too, has been tested in every way that we are. So we can approach Him with confidence and find understanding, mercy, and grace in our times of need (see Hebrews 4:14).

How has this made a difference in my life?

I have found that no matter what I am feeling or experiencing, Jesus understands. He Himself felt that very same emotion in His life. There is no emotion I have that He did not experience. When I was overwhelmed by the exhaustion of sibling rivalry, I asked,

*Where did Jesus experience the frustration that I have with these two kids?* And I thought of how the disciples argued about who was going to sit beside Him in the kingdom. Even He, the Son of God, had to deal with sibling rivalry.

The year that both Susy and Libby got married, all of my kids were to be with their in-laws for Christmas. For the first time in my life, I was going to be alone. A friend said, "Oh, you can have some special romantic times with John." She forgot that John is a pastor, and pastors are not home much at Christmas. It is a high-stress season for them. Roasting chestnuts by a romantic fire is not going to happen. The Hallmark version of Christmas just doesn't ring true. That my nest was going to be empty was glaringly painful.

Christmas Eve I curled up by myself on the couch. John was still at church for the last of three services. In my loneliness I went to the Scriptures and looked again at these principles revealed to the Hebrews.

How and when did Jesus experience what I'm feeling? Could God really understand what my empty nest *feels* like at Christmas? And then I thought about *His* first Christmas, when He sent His only Son—with whom He'd created the earth and everything in it and with whom He'd enjoyed constant fellowship—away to be born as a baby in a stable. He chose to empty His "nest" and to send His Son to be born in order to die. And in the process He knew His Son would be rejected and scorned, and suffer an excruciating death on the cross all because of His love for me. I had never before thought of Christmas Eve from God's perspective. And for the first time, I understood a tiny bit of what Christmas cost God. I will never forget that Christmas, because He encouraged me in a way no one else could. It is good to run to God in our loneliness.

### 3. *Find Some Friends*

A few years ago the two of us were attending a conference in Florida. When we finally had free time, we took a long walk on the beach with our friend Mary. As we walked, we began to ask each other, "What has been going on in your life? Is there a theme of the past year? What have you been thinking, learning, or struggling with?"

All three of us were in different phases of the empty nest. We were all busy with lots of acquaintances in our lives. Yet at the core, each of us felt lonely. We realized that what we longed for was to reconnect with some other women. In a way we felt we'd put deep female friendships on hold for several years as we focused on our kids.

It was now time to move out of that isolation and into community.

Joy had a similar experience. A mother of four and a well-known speaker, she had a meltdown when her last child left. She felt like her identity had just walked out the door. Even though she and her husband were unusually close, she knew he couldn't really relate to how she was feeling. She needed some other women; they would understand. Joy decided to be proactive. She called up thirteen women she'd known off and on over the years, and together they went away for a weekend. Simply being able to share honestly what was going on in her life and listening to other women made her feel not so silly. And it actually helped her feel normal again.

We need to run to God, we need to draw closer to our husbands, but we also need friends. Friends take the pressure off our marriages. Too often we look to our husbands to meet needs they were not created to meet—needs for which we should be going to God first. In addition, when we spend time with friends, our relationships with our husbands will benefit because the pressure is off of them to feel completely responsible for our happiness.

Recognizing that we need friends is a crucial step toward discovering the blessings of this empty-nest season. "But," you may be asking, "how do I find these friends?"

## Seven Tips for Reengaging With Women

The following seven tips will be helpful as you take a step toward reengaging with women.

### 1. Pray!

Pray that God would make you a good friend to others. Ask Him to lead you to one or two "soul sisters" for mutual encouragement.

### 2. Take the First Step

Make a list of several women you would like to get to know. Get together for lunch or coffee, and ask them questions about themselves. Two categories are helpful in conversation: relationships and schedules. Everyone has a schedule: *What is a typical week like for you? Do you have any projects that you are working on at the moment?* These are schedule questions. Relationship questions might include *I'd love to hear about your family. Is there anyone that you especially enjoy spending time with at the office, in your church, in your neighborhood?* Other good questions include *What's something you'd like to do that you haven't had time for? Is there a book that you've read that you have really enjoyed? What person has had an impact on your life and how?* Take some time and develop a list of good questions to use in getting to know people.

### 3. Be Persistent

You may feel that you didn't really click with the gal you had coffee with last week. That's okay. Just ask someone else. Keep at it. Developing close friendships takes time. Most relationships will remain at the acquaintance level. A few will have the potential to go deep. Don't give up because one or two get-togethers didn't turn out the way you hoped they would.

### 4. Be Open

It's healthy to have friendships with different types of people. We need all sorts of people in our lives—old, young, rich, poor, people of different races, and those with different theological, political, and educational backgrounds. There's no room for snobbery in the kingdom of God, and God Himself may choose someone to be your friend that you wouldn't ordinarily pick.

### 5. Be Wise

When a relationship moves from the acquaintance level to a deeper type of friendship, we need to be wise. It's all too easy to hang out with a bunch of women who—intentionally or unintentionally—"bash" their husbands. We need to be women who are *for* each other's marriages and who are encouraging one another to a deeper commitment to our husbands. We need women in our lives who are willing to say, "I don't think you are being fair to your husband. What are you doing to move closer to him?" This is accountability. This type of friendship develops with trust and a sense of vulnerability. It takes time to get to this level of friendship, but it is well worth it. And we need it.

### 6. Be Forgiving

It's important that we keep short accounts in relationships. We must not be demanding: *You aren't spending time with me.* Rather than being possessive, choose to believe the best: *She has a lot on her plate right now.* Always give the benefit of the doubt. Don't assume that because she didn't speak to you that she's mad at you. She may have had a bad day. You don't know everything that she's dealing with. Be loyal—stand up for her and stick with her.

### 7. Develop a Servant's Heart

It has been said that there are two kinds of people: One walks into the room with an attitude of *Here I am, please care for me,* and the other walks in with the attitude *There you are, how can I care for you?* We want to be "there you are" women who seek to reach out to others.

We are all shy to some degree, and at times we fear rejection. It's easy to blame others for our loneliness. Instead, we must seek to become "there you are" women, serving others. Practice the art of encouragement. Send a note or email just to say, "I'm thinking about you and praying for your day." Cook double and take a meal to a stressed-out friend.

One of the great blessings of the empty nest is that we now have time to hang out with friends. If we are out of practice, it may be awkward at first, but take the plunge. There are rich relationships out there for you, and the joy that is waiting for you in "girl time" is amazing.

We've found it to be one of the best cures for loneliness.

> "The Lord your God is with you, the Mighty Warrior who saves. He will take great delight in you; in his love he will no longer rebuke you, but will rejoice over you with singing."
>
> Zephaniah 3:17 NIV

## Take the Next Step

•  •  •  •  •

1. How has loneliness shown itself in your life?

2. Which of the seven steps might you take this week to connect with other women?

3. Often a cure for loneliness is caring for someone else. Is there someone that you can reach out to today with encouragement? How will you do it?

**Recommended Reading**

*Over Salad and Hot Bread: What an Old Friend Taught Me About Life* by Mary Jenson (Howard Books, 2006)

# Helen's Story

## One Day, One Hour at a Time

Education has always been a priority for Helen and Paul. Growing up in the Philippines, they observed the opportunities a good education provides, and they wanted that for their children.

When their first child was born, they moved to Hawaii. In time they were blessed with three children. Paul was involved in theater, and Helen in education, including teaching and advising graduate students.

Helen explains,

> When our children were born, we gave them back to God. We realized that they were His and we were merely His stewards. Our job was to do our best to take care of them for Him. Our guiding principle was "Train up a child in the way he should go, even when he is old he will not depart from it" (Proverbs 22:6 NASB). For us that meant teaching them to love God and helping them to receive a good education.
>
> My husband and I were filled with joy through the years watching our children develop character even through their growing pains and our stumbling along in raising them. We knew when the time came that they were well equipped to fly on their own. However, we failed to equip ourselves to let go of them!
>
> Although I knew independence was right, it came back to haunt me when our first child got ready to graduate from high school. All of his senior year, I'd look him in the face and realize he was leaving soon, and I'd burst into tears! I was grateful that I still had two more children left under our roof and resolved that I would be stronger the second time around. That didn't happen. Even when our third left, I cried for a week. And they all chose to go to colleges in the northeast, six thousand miles away! They *had* become independent, but now I wasn't so sure I liked it!

As Helen coped with the empty nest, she realized that she needed to focus on others rather than herself and how she was feeling. But first she had some good cries.

It's important to have a friend who will let you cry it out—a friend who will simply be there and hug you. This was very therapeutic for me. Then you need to get over it and get on with life.

In order to move from my pity party, I made a renewed effort to reach out to others. I've found it helpful to focus on the other person—to ask questions about what she is doing, how she is doing, what is on her plate.

Helen and Paul have always used their home as an oasis to care for others. When they moved to a new neighborhood, it wasn't long before they took the initiative to get to know their neighbors, inviting them for dinner or dessert or to a weekly Bible study they hosted. With the kids gone, they explored new ways of using hospitality.

"You have to look at how God has made you and ask: What is my particular bent? What do I love? How might God use this? I love people and I love simply being available," Helen remarks.

God is using Helen in numerous ways. When a friend needed help cleaning out her home, Helen was there. When a neighbor was open to walking, Helen was available. Juggling teaching, volunteer commitments, and needs of others can be overwhelming, but Helen's approach is to take one day at a time. Her prayer is simple yet profound: "God, show me how you want to use me today, and help me to obey you joyfully." The empty nest can be a long season, but it is lived only one day and sometimes one hour at a time.

As Helen reflects on her empty nest and her new freedom, she says,

When we understand that we have always been simply God's stewards of our kids, it's easier to let them go. We have the assurance that they are protected and gently held in the loving arms of Jesus. We will always be their parents in the different stages of their lives. Loving God, our children, and others will always be in season.

# *Chapter 4*

## What Do I Do
## With My Disappointments?

Life wouldn't be so hard if we didn't expect it to be
so easy.

Mick Yoder

What do you do when you finish the race of full-time mother-hood but find your hoped-for celebration cut short by some loss? A child has rejected your values or dropped out of school; is on drugs, pregnant, or in prison; or has run away. He has no interest in finishing school, getting a job, or living responsibly. Maybe an illness or disorder is involved. These are the real life situations of some of our friends.

And what if the fault line runs not through your parenting but through your marriage? You suddenly realize that your life's partner is not with you at the finish line. You look to him and are painfully aware that your marriage is empty, dull, isolated, and lonely. Instead of expectancy for the future, you are feeling a sense of apprehension about being alone with your husband again. One woman said with a clear sense of fright in her voice, "What will I do with him?"

Perhaps now that you find yourself in middle age, you are bewildered at your loss of youth, the discovery of lines and wrinkles, aches and pains, and physical diminishments of every kind. The vibrancy, vitality, and energy of youth are clearly waning. The clock is ticking. Perhaps you, like many of us, are halfway to a hundred! Oh my, that is a staggering thought. How did this happen so quickly?

Paul David Tripp writes in his book *Lost in the Middle*:

> We are disappointed because we age. We are dissatisfied because our dreams slipped out of our hands. We are discouraged that, in our sin, we failed many, many times. We are disappointed that good things come to an end and that people move on. Midlife exposes how much we struggle with the fact that God completes His work of redemption in us by keeping us in the middle of all of the harsh realities of the fall.[1]

When you were young, you were an idealist. Life would work out. You planned and hoped for a great future. But reality is often different. Now, today, you are faced with the results of mistakes you made with your kids, your husband, your friends, your family, your body. Regrets over all the "could haves" and "should haves" may be screaming at you. You had one shot at this job called family and life, and it has not worked out as you had planned.

*Disappointment* is sadness over the losses of life. And we all have them. We have discovered in talking to hundreds of women that the majority of us arrive at the empty nest with one or more significant losses in some area of our lives. Loss and disappointment are part of the journey.

## A Prodigal

BARBARA: One of my daughters chose a road for her life that we never would have foreseen or imagined in the sweet, delightful, innocent days of her childhood. Her life-altering choices significantly affected Dennis and me and our other children, bringing us much grief and disappointment. As a result, my transition into the empty nest was hardly a joyous experience. Perhaps you can identify.

My daughter began making some minor but nonetheless poor choices during her sixth-grade year. By the time she was a senior in high school, she had spiraled into depression, dropped out of school, left home to live with a friend (who was not someone we approved of), and was making poor lifestyle choices that were no longer minor.

In those six years, Dennis and I worked through the whole range of options available to parents of teens who rebel in serious ways: counseling for us and for her, interventions, prayer and fasting, more rules, fewer rules, contracts, and endless conversations as a couple and with her that left us at the end of her eighteenth year exhausted, discouraged, and feeling a profound sense of defeat.

Our situation made our home a gloomy place to be on prom night, awards night, and graduation day. Other seniors and their parents and families were celebrating achievements while we were sitting at home alone. Disappointed.

We suddenly felt "divorced" from everyone, excommunicated from this community of friends. The parents of her classmates at school and church were not a part of our lives anymore. Added to this was our worry, because often we didn't even know where our daughter was or if she was safe. Our hopes and dreams for this child had vaporized. As parents, we felt left behind.

And not only did we suffer a sense of parental failure and loss because of our daughter's choices, we also discovered we had some hollow places in our marriage because we'd been working so diligently on her problems that we had little left to give to each other. We were tired and fragile and weakened by the experience. It was a lonely, scary, and sad place to be.

## Catherine's Cancer

Catherine's approach to the empty nest was marred by a different type of hardship.

The summer before our last child left home for college, I was diagnosed with cancer and was told I needed immediate treatment. My first question to the doctor was, "Can I delay this treatment until I get my daughter settled in college this fall?" His response was, "We should have started yesterday, but I'll give you a week." This was a huge blow. I knew what it was like to send a child off to college, but this was my last one. I had planned to do a great job with her—stay to help decorate her room, walk around campus and show her where her classes were—all the things I'd not been able to do with the other children because of the demands at home.

Weeks later my husband and I took her to the university. I had a mask on and was bald. When we left, my daughter cried and I felt guilty and very sad. I felt like I had cheated her.

For the first few months, everything seemed to go smoothly for me with my treatment and for my daughter with school, but I began to sense that she was only telling me the good things that were going on, hoping not to upset me. By the midpoint of her second semester, she and I were both in a downward spiral. I had dropped out of Bible study; she had started skipping classes. I was withdrawing from my husband and friends; she changed friends and quit calling home as often. I was feeling ugly. She blew her budget.

Even though my husband was not able to engage with me emotionally in this part of my life (both the illness and the empty nest), he knew something had to be done for both of us. When our daughter came home for spring break, he had an honest, straightforward talk with us. Then we all prayed together. Deep down our daughter was tired of being unsettled and confused. She was acting out due to this, and I needed to hear what my husband said to her, too. We both needed someone to say, "You've got to quit this right now." I don't think either of us had the foresight or energy to get out of the pit we were in. I know that God was working through my husband's love and concern for us, plus his prayer changed our perspective.

Now I thank God for that dark time. Our daughter has told us many times that she learned so much from that period in her life and our life as a family. When I look back at my illness and the empty nest happening at the same time, I think, *I'm so glad God was in control.* The guilt I felt because I could not do the empty nest right got all mixed up with my illness. As I got better physically, I also healed emotionally. And I've had the opportunity to see my family pull together and help each other, even during the times we've struggled.

## Interruptions

Shirley entered the empty nest with a series of changes that spelled loss for her in very different ways. In the first year of her empty nest, she experienced menopause in earnest. Then she and her husband sold their home and moved—not to another city or even another state, but to a foreign country. Shirley said, "I scored big points on the stress scale!" Everything that was familiar and dear was an ocean away. What had sounded exciting and adventurous became lonely and depressing.

Your disappointment may not be a wayward child or a life-threatening illness or a move overseas. You may instead be experiencing another kind of interruption, like Sue, who lost both of her parents and started menopause in the first four months of her empty-nest season. The change may be an unexpected career shift like Mary experienced when she realized her passion for her part-time work had evaporated, leaving her floundering and confused. Or your loss may be that of diminished youthfulness and energy, like Carol.

Carol was menopausal and had shoulder surgery right before her last child left for college. It left her unable to do much of her normal everyday work. She said,

> My husband did the cooking and cleaning because I could not move my left arm or lift anything. I went to physical therapy for nine months. I also experienced much fatigue and some forgetfulness. During this time, I read a book that I had heard about on the *FamilyLife Today* radio program called *The Menopause Manager*.[2] It was very helpful for me. I explained many of the things to my husband as I worked through the book so he would understand little by little. Now, years later, we are still working through the effects

of menopause on our relationship. We are continuing to adjust, to grow in understanding about intimacy, and to balance my workload at the office and at home.

Whatever the source of disappointment in your life, there are perspectives and solutions that can make a difference in your ability to move forward with grace rather than getting stuck in the quicksand of sadness. The question is how to move on with this new kind of life that involves loss.

## Google Earth

Moving forward from a place of disappointment begins by gaining perspective. If you've ever used Google Earth, you know it allows you to zoom out to a satellite view of any spot in the world. From that vantage point, all that crowds and blocks our view is taken away and only the big picture remains. We see Earth from the fringes of heaven. Sometimes we need to see life in the same way.

Nineteenth-century Bible scholar F. B. Meyer made this statement: "Earthly prosperity is no sign of the special love of heaven; nor are sorrow and care any mark of God's disfavor."[3] How easy it is to assume that loss and pain mean God has turned His back on us, when that is never the case.

BARBARA: In the darkest days of personal suffering from the effects of my daughter's choices, I taped a small card to my steering wheel on which I'd written James 1:2–4: "Consider it all joy, my brethren, when you encounter various trials, knowing that the testing of your faith produces endurance. And let endurance have its perfect result, that you may be perfect and complete, lacking in nothing."

I read those words over and over to remind myself of God's perspective and purpose in the midst of great loss. Even though I felt no joy at all, I focused repeatedly on the phrase "knowing that the testing of your faith produces endurance" to remind myself that the unseen character quality of endurance was going to come from this time of testing even though it could not be seen in the present.

I learned that the greatest expression of personal faith is when an individual continues to believe in God and chooses to trust Him even when circumstances are extremely difficult. The words of the Bible became life and strength and hope to me in those days as I purposed to "look not at the things which are seen, but at the things which are not seen" (2 Corinthians 4:18).

In the midst of any trial or struggle or time of loss, there is always a larger view of life and what God intends. Every time, the difficulty lies in moving our eyes from a self-focused inward perspective up to God's eternal perspective. There is a profound principle of life that says, "God is not so concerned about my happiness as He is about my holiness." That statement is a reminder of the big picture of what God is up to when He allows difficulty in life. He is building character and holiness, compassion and understanding, perseverance and endurance in our hearts.

Here are some of the other verses in the Bible that helped me through this hard time:

1. "The Lord supports the afflicted" (Psalm 147:6).
2. "The Lord is near to the brokenhearted" (Psalm 34:18).
3. One of the most well-known Scriptures of all is Psalm 23, which reminded me that when I walk "through the valley of the shadow of death, I will fear no evil: for thou art with me" (v. 4 KJV).
4. From the heart of a man named Job, who suffered more loss than most of us will ever know, comes this famous quote: "Though He slay me, I will hope in Him" (Job 13:15).

Ultimately, God wants us to know Him. He loves us supremely, and His great purposes always have that end in mind. In his book *Shattered Dreams*, Larry Crabb writes, "The suffering caused by shattered dreams must not be thought of as something to relieve if we can or endure if we must. It's an opportunity to be embraced, a chance to discover our desire for the highest blessing God wants to give us, an encounter with Himself."[4]

While I still wish my daughter had chosen a responsible, healthy way of life as a teenager, I can say with complete honesty that I am grateful for both my precious daughter and the experience of her wanderings, because my husband and I have grown so much in our faith. I have experienced significant encounters with the living God that make all the suffering worth it. I wouldn't go back to knowing God as I did before. The richness of today makes yesterday's relationships empty by comparison.

And today, fifteen years after she dropped out of school, our daughter is mom to two sweet daughters and a loyal and committed wife to her husband of thirteen years. Together they are a picture of God's amazing love and grace. It is His grace that has worked this redemption story, not mine.

## Accept That What's Done Is Done

Elisabeth Kübler-Ross did groundbreaking research in the 1960s on the subject of death and dying. The results of her work now form the basis for recognizing the common stages of grief: denial, anger, bargaining, depression, and acceptance. The last of her five stages, acceptance, is important for women in the empty-nest season.

To accept what has been done means we have to let go over and over and over. We desperately want to fix things to ease our own pain, but so often we can't. The very best thing is to let go so that God can do what only He can do. As Martin Luther King Jr. said, "We must accept finite disappointment, but we must never lose infinite hope."[5] So how do we accept less than ideal circumstances?

### *Live in the Present*

We have both learned a simple principle: We cannot change the past, but we can control how we respond to it in the present, whether it is in relation to our children, our husbands, or our own choices and circumstances. Dealing with any kind of loss presents us with questions we must answer if we are to move on:

1. Will I trust God with my child's choices—her depression, his failures?
2. Will I believe He has good in mind with my child's handicap, his loss of motivation for college and career, her decisions that do not reflect our values?
3. Will I accept where I am physically, knowing that the health and vitality I do have are gifts from God?
4. Will I work to persevere and grow in my marriage in the midst of my disappointments?
5. Will I accept the limitations of my job situation, knowing that God is still in control?
6. Will I accept what has been done—the results of choices in the past—and move forward?

### Give Thanks in All Things

A short verse in the Bible that is easy to quote but difficult to practice is "Give thanks in all circumstances" (1 Thessalonians 5:18 ESV). It doesn't say to give thanks in the happy things or the carefree things or the good things. It also doesn't say to give thanks *for* all things. The word used to describe which things is *all*. So we are to give thanks *in* the midst of all things. And that means the happy and *sad*, carefree and *difficult*, good and *bad* things in life. What enables us to do this? Simply knowing that God is *with us* in the midst of "all things." No matter what is happening, we can express thanks; and as we do, we can experience His supernatural peace.

### Make and Keep Your Marriage a Priority

Chapter 5 is devoted to this most important relationship of all, but for now we want to say that enduring difficulty together as a couple can ultimately be a wonderful opportunity to see your marriage grow deeper and to develop an intimacy not possible otherwise. And we both know from personal experience that it's not easy. Making a marriage last for a lifetime is hard work; it means that you can't quit. The choice must continually be made to move into new levels of transparency, which requires risk. The alternative to keeping your marriage a priority in the empty nest is a greater likelihood of divorce.

The *New York Times* reported on the rise of divorce among older Americans:

> Late-life divorce (also called "silver" or "gray" divorce) is becoming more common, and more acceptable. In 2014, people age 50 and above were twice as likely to go through a divorce than in 1990, according to the National Center for Family and Marriage Research at Bowling Green State University in Ohio. For those over 65, the increase was even higher.[6]

Sadly, Marie understands this new divorce trend firsthand. The year she turned fifty, her last child left home and her husband wanted a divorce. The proceedings were final very quickly, and she found herself alone, searching for a place to live and for a job so she could make ends meet. She said she would go to work, return to her tiny one-room apartment, and cry herself to sleep every night. She shared her experience, saying, "I felt so alone with no family. I had to learn to let my expectations die about being married for the rest of my life. And I had to learn to trust God even though I was bitterly disappointed. I knew I had no other choice."

According to an AARP (American Association of Retired Persons) report, "Compared to other losses that may occur at midlife or older, people age 40 and older generally feel that divorce is more emotionally devastating than losing a job, about equal to experiencing a major illness, and somewhat less devastating than a spouse's death."[7] The DivorceCare ministry curriculum says that for every four years of marriage, it takes one year to get over the loss of divorce of a spouse.[8] Ending a marriage is never easy, but at this stage of life, it will be an even more difficult journey. Lisa says she only started to be happy again after seven years, as she learned to find, as she says, "treasures hidden in the darkness" (Isaiah 45:3 NLT).

### Get Wise Counsel From Someone Who Has Been Where You Are

One of the greatest sources of comfort in times of suffering and loss is the companionship of those who have been where you are and who can really understand. This is one of the reasons Alcoholics Anonymous and Al-Anon have been so successful. These organizations bring people with similar struggles together, where they find help and hope. Again, as suggested in chapter 3, we encourage you to reach out to other women to meet for lunch or coffee and share your lives with one another. We need to comfort one another and be comforted, but unless we make those needs known, we will suffer alone.

## For the Many Who Will Never Be Empty Nesters

In talking to so many wonderful women while researching this book, it has become abundantly clear that this concept of an empty nest is really a very modern idea. The privilege of living independently in marriage for a second season is not common in much of the world today. In most countries, several generations share living quarters. Our Western concept of an empty nest being part of the normal rhythm of life is rather new in this world. But it's not normal at all to many of the women we interviewed.

### Living With Adult Special-Needs Children

Three of our friends each have an adult special-needs child who likely will never be able to live on their own. All three of these moms have done so much for these children, seeking therapies and vocational training in hopes of giving them the best opportunities for some level of independence. But even with all their heroic work, these three (and many others) may have to plan for a long-term living relationship with their adult special-needs children.

Cindi wrote:

> Unless we find a group home suitable for our son and a place we'd feel comfortable leaving him, which is not our desire or plan at this time, we will be facing the "never-empty nest." There are times that we feel the sting of having our wings clipped, knowing we will probably never experience the *real* empty nest. It's sometimes difficult, as our friends begin this time of life, to realize we can't pick up and join them without scheduling care for our adult special-needs son. It often eliminates us from being a part of what we thought would be a very special time for just the two of us. God knew our time would be special in very different ways than we had planned. As we surrender our plan to His, He will help us make whatever adjustments will be necessary.

### Raising Grandchildren

And then there are many empty-nest women who are raising their grandchildren.

Grace wrote:

> Our daughter became a single mom when she gave birth to her own daughter, Noelle. From the beginning Noelle spent a lot of time with us. She came to our home on the weekends her mother had to work, and she came whenever she was sick. When she started school, she spent all of her vacations, including summers, with us.
>
> When our daughter decided to get her master's degree, the three of us decided that Noelle would move in with us until the degree work was completed. The transition back to full-time parenting has not been seamless for my husband and me. Getting back into the school routine and all that it involves has been demanding for both of us as I now find myself in the pickup line at her school at 2:45 every afternoon.
>
> There have been other adjustments as well. After raising our own children, we looked forward to the years of the empty nest as much as anyone else. We liked the freedom of deciding on the spur of the

moment to join our friends for dinner or a movie. Over time we have noticed that people don't call us as much for social interaction, as they know we are not always available because of other obligations related to Noelle's life. And we're more tired in the evenings than we used to be. We just can't do all that we did when our own children were young.

We don't resent our circumstances. We offered to do this for our daughter. We chose it. And though there are sacrifices, we know that we couldn't be doing anything more important with our lives. Certainly it is a privilege to be so intimately involved with Noelle on a daily basis. We have an opportunity to know her in ways that we won't have with other grandchildren. We adore Noelle, and she is truly a gift to us in every way.

As in every season of life, we have found that once decisions about priorities have been made, we must be single-minded in carrying out those priorities. We can't live two lives; we have chosen to live as parents of a young child again. That means our lives cannot look like the lives of our empty-nest friends. For us to try to live in both worlds or to wish that things were different will only cause stress, frustration, and less energy for the job at hand. We know that life is worthwhile and satisfying only when we give it away, and we are trusting that our efforts during these short years will contribute in positive ways as Noelle develops physically, emotionally, mentally, and spiritually.

### Caring for Aging Parents

And of course there is the common interruption of caring for aging parents that often occurs at the same time as the empty nest.

Silvia's mother came to live with her and her husband. She shared with us:

My husband and I both felt it was better to have her with us than for me to continue flying to her home many times a year. Also, he knew I'd be worried about her more than ever since she's nearly blind and was now alone. It has been an ongoing adjustment. She will need assistance more and more as time goes on. I guess we see the empty nest as a myth. It certainly isn't what we anticipated. However, we both believe taking care of my mother is the mission God has called us to at this time. It's funny, but I remember waiting for a grandparent to come take care of the kids so my husband and I could have a night off. Now we wait for a grandchild to come take care of my mom so we can have a night off!

## Experiencing Loss Is Normal

Arriving at the empty nest with grief and loss is not so very unusual, nor is it abnormal to face interruptions or difficulties. It may feel that way as we look from afar at other apparently carefree couples our age who seem to be joyously entering this season. But that is part of the problem. We always see others from afar. Our conclusions about another's happiness may not be accurate at all.

But God, in His great wisdom, love, and grace, always works toward us as individuals with redemption in mind. He is always eager to refine us and draw us closer to Him. Oftentimes we have realized He is trying to gently loosen our grasp from those things we hold too tightly, in order to prepare us for heaven.

In *Lost in the Middle*, Tripp says,

> God fights for us with the full might of his redemptive hand. He is willing to make us uncomfortable and sad. He is willing to bring us through suffering and grief. He is willing to shake and unsettle us. He is willing to squash our dreams and let the air out of our hopes. He is willing to let what we have craved slip like sand through our fingers. And he does all of these things because we are precious to him. We are the apple of his eye. He will not share us with another. He will not allow us to live in the delusion that we have found elsewhere what can only be found in him.[9]

Whatever disappointment may be yours as you enter the empty nest, remember that God is still in control, what's done is done, and in giving thanks in all things, we express faith that God can bring good out of our losses.

> Therefore we do not lose heart, but though our outer
> man is decaying, yet our inner man is being renewed

day by day . . . while we look not at the things which are seen, but at the things which are not seen; for the things which are seen are temporal, but the things which are not seen are eternal.

2 Corinthians 4:16, 18

# Take the Next Step

· · · · ·

Have you been disappointed as often in life as we have? If you are like us, you, too, have hoped in things that will not completely satisfy: people, circumstances, health, material things, etc. There is a verse in the Bible that is startling in its simplicity and boldness: *"Hope does not disappoint*, because the love of God has been poured out within our hearts through the Holy Spirit who was given to us" (Romans 5:5, emphasis ours). It is an amazing thought to ponder—that there is a hope that will never disappoint us.

Identify who and what has so often brought disappointment to your life. Reduce your expectations of these people and circumstances, and then increase your hope in God alone. He will not disappoint!

- *People:* Make a list of those people you are hoping will make you happy or those you have looked to for happiness. Who has disappointed you?
- *Circumstances:* What circumstances are bringing you dissatisfaction in life (e.g., aging parents' health, financial investments, government leaders, even weather or traffic conditions, etc.)? What is disappointing you now?
- *Personal Expectations:* What personal failures or potential changes produce vacillating happiness and discontent in your

67

life (e.g., losing weight, finding that miracle wrinkle cream, buying that longed-for item, etc.)? What about yourself has disappointed you?

- *The Future:* Do you find yourself thinking, *When this happens, life will be better?* For example, when our children were babies, we couldn't wait for them to be out of diapers so life would be easier. Then we couldn't wait for them to talk so they could tell us what was wrong. Then we couldn't wait for . . . What is it today? What are you hoping for that might not ever happen?
- *Misconceptions About God:* As humans, we sometimes try to reduce God and His Word to a formula that says if I do this for God, He will do this for me. Are you hoping He will be like Cinderella's fairy godmother to you, granting whatever you wish? Which of your views of God have disappointed you? Remember, God wants us to hope in Him alone for who He is, not who we wish Him to be.

Now that you have identified some of your disappointments, are there any steps that you need to take *in order to be released from them?* For example, is there someone you need to forgive or apologize to? Do you need to pray, acknowledging these disappointments to God and asking Him to enable you to overcome them? Are there Bible verses that you could memorize that would help you focus your thoughts where they need to be?

## Recommended Reading

*A Grace Disguised: How the Soul Grows Through Loss* by Jerry Sittser (Zondervan, 2004)

*Where Is God When It Hurts?* by Philip Yancey (Zondervan, 2002)

*Lost in the Middle: Midlife and the Grace of God* by Paul David Tripp (Shepherd Press, 2004)

*When God Interrupts: Finding New Life Through Unwanted Change* by M. Craig Barnes (InterVarsity Press, 1996)

# Julia's Story

## Dogs and Decorating

As a single parent, Julia faced unique challenges when she entered the empty nest.

For nearly fifteen years she'd balanced work with raising her two children. In addition, she had several postgraduate students living in her home. Her career path had ranged from communications and broadcasting to freelance writing and public relations. She had also become involved as a volunteer with Guiding Eyes for the Blind by taking in puppies and socializing them in preparation for advanced training as guide dogs. (If you dropped by Julia's home, you would be greeted by a chorus of puppies under the direction of her golden retriever, Brinkley.)

As her youngest child prepared to leave home, Julia was about to turn fifty-five. While many of her friends were considering retirement, she was contemplating a new career.

She said,

> Because I'd been a single parent with a busy career for years, I saw the empty nest more like a fresh opportunity—I began to assess my priorities. I wanted a job with flexibility so I could still be available to my kids. I also had to be realistic about the fact that I was the sole financial provider and needed to think about retirement one day. Being a single parent, I'd been forced to learn to plan ahead, so to do this again was not all that unusual for me.

With these priorities in mind, Julia took some time to examine what she had done in her life and to consider what she was interested in for the future. Without leaving her job, she began to explore the field of decorating to assess the possibility of reviving an old interest. She made a short-term commitment to work for a designer to learn all she could; then she started her own business, which provides the finances she needs while allowing her the freedom to visit her kids.

And she still trains guide dogs. Julia explains, "Training the dogs is my calling. Decorating is my necessity."

She also has young interns from her church live in her home. "The involvement with these young adults has encouraged me and has given my children positive role models to look up to. My son particularly benefited by being exposed to godly young men several years older than he was. They gave him a picture of what he could become."

Julia is not afraid of the changes she's discovering in the empty nest.

There have been so many times in the past that I have panicked about what would happen to me and the children. But when I take the time to look back, I see God's faithfulness to me. I also see that He often worked out things very differently from how I thought He would. My life has been full of unexpected twists, but God's ways have proven to be the best way for me.

*Chapter 5*

# How Do I Relate
# to My Husband Now?

To have and to hold from this day forward, for better, for
worse, for richer, for poorer, in sickness and in health,
to love and to cherish, till death do us part.

The Solemnization of Matrimony
from *The Book of Common Prayer*

**B**ess and Gary couldn't wait for the empty nest. Raising their
kids had been tough. They'd had different approaches to discipline, had struggled on a tight budget, and had postponed many
of their dreams in order to be with their kids. Now the last one was
leaving, and they felt they had done the best they could. Finally,
they were about to be free from the daily stresses of parenting.
They were excited. They couldn't wait for it to be "just us" again.

Shelly's situation was just the opposite. She had poured her life
into her kids; they had come first. Now, as the last child got ready
to leave, she was scared, really scared. "I don't even feel like I know
my husband. I haven't been alone with him since I was twenty-six.

Our whole life has revolved around the kids. Now what will we talk about at the dinner table? What will we do on weekends? I don't even know if I have energy left to put into this relationship. And I don't know if I want to."

When our kids leave, we are forced to consider our marriage in a new light. This can be wonderful or it can be scary. We may be thrilled as we look forward to a second honeymoon season with our husband. Or we may be asking ourselves, *Without the kids, do we have enough to hold us together?*

Most likely, we'll respond with a mixture of both fear and excitement. Yet at some point we will wonder, *What will my marriage look like now?* Anticipating the hurdles in the road ahead is essential to a good marriage in the empty-nest season.

As I (Susan) approached the empty nest, I realized I hadn't given much thought to how it would impact my marriage. I was too busy trying to empty the nest! Yet as I began to think about John, I realized there were two traps that I could easily fall into and needed to avoid.

I knew it would be easy for me to expect John to fill the emotional void left by the kids. Subconsciously, I could expect him to spend more time with me, to talk more with me, to empathize with me, to give me a sense of purpose. Unwittingly, I could look to him to make me happy. And of course I'd expect him to understand. When he let me down, I'd become critical and dissatisfied with him and with our marriage.

Back when I was raising little kids, I'd learned how easy it is for a married woman to look to her husband to meet all her needs—to appreciate her, affirm her, listen to her, understand her, and build her up. But God did not create any man who could meet all of those needs. I realized that too often we, as women, look to our men to meet needs that we should be going to God first to meet. I'd learned that truth in the early years of our marriage, and I realized I would need to practice it again in this season.

A second trap that I knew I had to watch out for was an attitude that said, *He can't understand my life now. He doesn't appreciate how different this season is for me. After all, he's busy, and with the kids gone, he'll have more time to work. I'll just have to carve out my own life. He can do his thing and I can do mine. We'll connect when we can.*

I knew this kind of attitude could create emotional distance and lead to a sense of isolation. I did need a fresh plan for my life, but we had to figure it out together.

## The Wild Card

Usually, this season is harder on women than on men. So much of our identity has been tied to being a mom. Even if we've had a career outside the home, it has been secondary to mothering, whereas men's primary identities come through their jobs. Even though they may take fatherhood seriously, their careers have been their primary calling. We're different. Women nurture; men provide and protect. On the surface, life may not seem to change that much for men when the nest empties. So you may be in for a surprise by the way your husband reacts. In fact, he may be the "wild card," as Jean found out.

Even though Jean's husband, Randy, is a busy executive, he has been intimately involved in his kids' lives. When his oldest boys got into music, he was at their concerts, traveling with them, advising them. When the youngest took up golf, he played with him and went to his tournaments. Communication was candid and constant around the dinner table. Time with the boys took priority over everything else. But then the last one graduated and went off to college. Randy felt at a loss but couldn't really verbalize it. His sadness came out in little ways, but Jean didn't realize the extent of his feelings until it affected a special date night they had planned. They were both excited, and Randy stopped to buy flowers on his way home. As he pulled into the drive, his cell phone rang. It was Tad, who had just left for college.

"Dad," he began in a sad voice, "it's been a bad day. I played a terrible round of golf in team practice. I feel so embarrassed."

By the time Randy opened the front door, he was in the dumps, too. Gone was the excitement of being with Jean. He just felt down—he couldn't fix things for his son. And that made him sad.

Jean's response was, "It's just a golf game. He'll get over it!"

Yes, Tad would get over it. In fact, he was probably over it by the time he hung up the phone. Often kids simply need to vent, and then they move on to something else. But the sadness stayed with Randy throughout the evening.

Often, we women are the ones impacted by the pitiful phone calls, but not always. Men have emotions, too.

Larry and Betsy found themselves in a similar situation. Because Betsy had been thinking and planning for the empty nest for several years, she was more prepared. During that last year she had intentionally enjoyed the final soccer game, the last prom—all those special events. Larry, on the other hand, wasn't really giving the future much thought. One of his traditions was to cook big Saturday breakfasts for the guys and their friends. An early morning person, he loved fixing a big spread. He relished interacting with the kids as they came over. It was a highlight for him. And then the kids left. And the first Saturday he moped. He didn't know what to do with himself. He was at a total loss. Betsy, however, was glad for the clean kitchen, the quiet, and a rare chance to curl up and read the paper in peace.

Another dad, Frank, had a completely different reaction. His three kids left at the same time. Grinning from ear to ear, he remarked, "When my kids moved out, my girlfriend [his wife] moved back in! The electricity bill went down, and the gas bill dropped. Now I have hot water for my shower. And there's hardly any trash to take out!"

Frank was clearly thrilled with this new season.

We can't always anticipate how we or our husbands will respond to the empty nest. It varies according to personality. Your best friend's reaction may be completely different from yours; and your husband's response, the opposite of her husband's. Your husband may not even be able to articulate what is going on inside of him.

That's okay. We need to be patient and give him grace, just as we want him to do for us.

In a way, marriage is like a dance. When we first get married, we learn how to dance together in one form. It may be awkward at first. The moves are hard to predict; we have different ways of doing things. Finally we get into step; then the first baby comes, and it's as if the music changed and we have to learn new steps. The music changes again in the teen years and again at the empty nest. We're still partners, but the new style of dancing is strangely unfamiliar. We have to work at getting in sync with each other, or our partnership will become distorted. It's a time of transition, and transitions are often clumsy.

Understanding a few things will help us to make sure that we stay in sync with our husbands.

## Husbands and Wives Grieve Differently

When Shelly's daughter left for college, Shelly became depressed. "I knew I was in trouble when I didn't want to get out of bed," she recalls. "Even though I *knew* better, I *felt* like I had no value. Who I was had just walked out the door. It was hard to talk to my husband about how I was feeling. He'd just want to fix things. I didn't need to be fixed; I needed him to listen!"

It's natural, and often admirable, that one spouse wants to *fix* the one who is grieving, but that is not always the best solution. You may need to keep your mouth closed and your ears—and heart—open. It may be helpful to ask, "Is this a time when you want some advice, or do you just need me to listen?" And then do what is requested. This can be difficult, because the parenting role often requires fixing things. But it's not your job to fix your spouse.

Usually, you will both grieve. But how you grieve will likely be different.

After dropping their son at college and starting the long drive home, both Seth and Becky felt a tremendous sadness. Seth's way of processing his grief was to talk. Becky, on the other hand, processed internally. Her silence made Seth feel that she wasn't sad and didn't care. Becky, however, was not only quietly processing her own grief but processing his verbal grief sentence by sentence. For her it was a double whammy—his talkativeness and her need for solitude.

It was a great help for the two of them to realize that they process differently—and therefore grieve differently. They had to learn to allow one another the freedom to grieve in their own way.

In some cases, a woman can become so focused on her own unhappiness that she fails to realize that her husband is grieving, too. His grief may not be so obvious.

Kelly found that she couldn't get her husband to go out. They used to be an active family when the kids were home. With them gone, she was ready to go on long bike rides and discover some new hiking trails, but he didn't want to. It took her a while to realize that his shutting down was a part of his grieving.

About the same time that their last child left, Susie's first one got married. Her husband quit his job without another prospect, and she hit menopause. By nature she was not an emotional person, but her system was on overload and tears flowed easily.

It was hard on her husband because he didn't know how to deal with her. Susie found it helpful to say to him, "Honey, I'm not always going to be like this. I will be all right again." Simply verbalizing what was going on alleviated unnecessary stress.

If we can talk about what we are feeling and going through together *while giving each other the freedom to respond differently,* we will be more likely to give and receive grace rather than to become critical or hurt.

## Relational Issues Will Resurface

The empty nest brings to the surface relational issues within your marriage that perhaps had been buried while you raised your kids—things you never dealt with in the tyranny of life or matters you let slide because you did not want a confrontation. Now that it is just the two of you again, some of these issues will resurface, and that can throw you for a loop.

Elsie had longed for her husband to communicate more openly, but communication had always been difficult for him, a reflective introvert. With children at home, family conversations flowed more naturally and Elsie was happier. But when the kids left, the silence seemed overwhelming. The problem of their communication gap became too obvious to ignore.

Paige's husband always had a hard time holding down a job. This made her feel insecure, but somehow they made it through the child-raising years. Then the empty nest arrived and he changed jobs again. Paige's own reaction made her realize that she needed help. She sought out a counselor, and with her help Paige began to realize that both her dad's leaving when she was a toddler and her mother's death when she was a teenager had contributed to her fears of abandonment—fears that were surfacing again in her relationship with her husband. With the help of a wise counselor, they were able to work through issues that had been set aside during the busy years of raising kids.

How you handle these resurrected issues is crucial. You can view them as opportunities to seek healing and to grow in your marriage, or as excuses to move toward isolation. Perhaps you need to initiate a conversation with your husband or even seek help from a counselor or trusted friend. Above all, remember that God is for your marriage and that nothing is impossible with Him (see Luke 1:37). He can redeem anything.

### Seasons of Transition Are Awkward

Moving into the empty-nest season is often an awkward transition. Like a coming storm, this unsettled time in life brings suitable conditions for conflict and misunderstanding. Why? Transitions make us vulnerable and irritable.

Perhaps you've had a rough day. A friend or colleague disappointed you, you missed a deadline, you wasted time doing things you didn't want to do, or your husband didn't follow through on something you'd counted on. In addition, you're lonely and missing the kids. Then your hubby comes in. He's had a frustrating day as well. He's tired and doesn't respond to you, and you react either by withdrawing or by blowing up. With no kids as a buffer, arguments get out of hand or you retreat into silence. Soon the two of you are into a good ol' fight or an estranged withdrawal. Left unresolved, bitterness begins to grow and you find yourself thinking, *We don't have a relationship anymore. I'm not even sure I like him.*

Sound familiar?

What has happened? You may have forgotten that transitions are tough.

When women first get married, everyone gives advice about newlywed adjustments. Then baby showers follow with advice from friends on the adjustments of being a mom. And then those teen years—friends with older kids enlighten those just entering that stage, and there are books to tell us that our challenges and our kids are usually normal. But in the empty nest, not many of our older friends have alerted us to the potential pitfalls.

## Three Common Pitfalls

As Christians we believe there is an enemy of our souls who wants our marriages to fall apart (see 1 Peter 5:8–9; Ephesians 6:10–18; 1 John 4:4). Part of the problem is not recognizing this enemy or his tactics. Instead, we think the problem is us or, more likely, our spouses.

In order to successfully transition your marriage into the empty-nest years, watch for three common pitfalls that many marriages face around this time: a critical spirit, emotional divorce, and affairs.

### 1. A Critical Spirit

How many middle-aged couples do you know who are still in love with each other and whose marriages you admire? Or said another way, How many do you know where there is criticism, condemnation, and alienation? Newlyweds seem to have cornered the market on being in love. And why is that? They usually have the time and focus. Empty-nest couples have the same two commodities; the challenge is to capitalize on them.

Oswald Chambers said, "The first thing that will hinder this joy is the captious irritation of thinking out circumstances."[1] *Captious* means quick to find fault. It is all too easy to fill the void left by the kids with criticism of our husbands. With the kids gone we tend to focus more on our spouses. It is easy to resent the way he is or is not, to find fault with what he has done or left undone, to revisit old wounds, to fret about the way we think things should be. Why do we wives do this? Partly because we are hurting and sad for our losses, partly because we know our husbands too well, partly because we have been mothering for so long that we switch our attention from our kids to our husbands without thinking. Unconsciously we become critical and don't even realize what we are doing. It's so subtle.

Once we do recognize what is happening, it's time to change course. Making changes can sometimes be as simple as deciding, *I make the choice to give my husband the benefit of the doubt, to not comment on everything he does or doesn't do, to focus on the things I appreciate about him, and to verbally express gratitude.*

### 2. Emotional Divorce

At different times in our lives, many of us will drift toward emotional divorce. It is so very common to arrive at the empty nest and feel some level of isolation. This has been true for both of us. During transitions we are especially vulnerable to this drift, as each spouse processes life's changes differently.

It might happen like this: *He's hurt me again. It's the same old thing. There's no use trying to talk it through. I just can't go there again. It's too exhausting, too painful. We'll live in the same house and carry on, but I can't keep trying. I can't share with him at a deep level anymore.*

Picture a glass patio door. It's like shutting the glass door on your marriage. You still see each other, but there's a barrier between you. This is emotional divorce—the road to isolation.

When you are pulled this way, recognize what is happening and make the decision to take a hammer and begin breaking the glass. How do you do this? Refuse to give in to the temptation to pull away from your husband, and instead, talk through the issues. Ask a wise couple whom you trust to talk with you, or get counseling if needed. Your marriage is too important to let it fade away. A thick glass panel doesn't crumble instantaneously. It takes constant chipping away until the barrier finally crumbles. In the same way, you have to be patient and chip away at your issues, knowing that God is for your marriage; He wants to remove the thick glass in order that fresh air might blow in and rejuvenate your marriage.

### 3. An Affair

Failing to stop the drift toward emotional divorce makes us increasingly vulnerable to an affair. Infidelity in women rarely takes place on the spur of the moment. Instead, these types of relationships usually begin with an emotional affair: *He understands me better than my husband does. He appreciates me in ways my husband does not. He finds me attractive. I am drawn to him. When we talk, I feel like he really listens to me.*

These comments were dropped in the middle of a conversation one morning as I (Susan) chatted with some women over coffee. The gal who shared these feelings was a committed believer, as was her husband. Because of the relationships between these women, this friend felt the freedom to share her temptation.

"Girls," she continued, "although nothing physical has happened yet, I know I'm treading on dangerous ground, and I know I need to sever this relationship. I need you to hold me accountable to do this."

As we continued to chat, her phone rang. Answering it, she turned aside and her face became ghostly white. We heard her say to the caller, "Please don't call me anymore. This relationship is not going in a healthy direction, and we need to end all connection now. Thank you and good-bye."

We sat in stunned silence. What an amazing God we have! How good of Him to have that man call her right at that moment when we were with her to provide the support she needed to end the relationship.

It's easy for us to let our fantasies rather than the truth lead us. It's helpful to ask ourselves, *Am I believing in a fantasy or seeking the truth?* God's Word says that we are to *flee from*, not *flirt with* temptation (see 1 Corinthians 6:18). We must run away from other men and run toward our husbands.

When driving a car, we are dependent upon road signs that signal speed limits, merging traffic, dangerous curves, and other warnings. These signs are in place for our safety. In a similar way, we are sharing these warnings about the road ahead for the safety of your marriage. We are both strongly for marriages thriving, not just surviving. Knowing what the dangers are is the better part of avoiding them.

We urge you to remember: Your spouse is not your enemy, he is your partner. You're on the same team.

### Preparing for a Great New Season in Your Marriage

If it is true that women change over the years as we have children, learn a new identity called mom, and become both enriched and transformed by the journey, then it is equally true that our husbands' identities and lives also change. As we've already said, no married couple remains the same two people they were when they said their "I dos."

So a fresh look at what it means to be a wife to this man of yours is needed. At this season it's easy to assume you've learned all that already, but remaining teachable is so crucial to a healthy marriage. We want to encourage and challenge you to keep your marriage strong by being as eager to be a good wife today as you were when you first began. So at this juncture we want to strongly encourage you to read Barbara's book *Letters to My Daughters: The Art of Being a Wife*. It is a call to every woman to create beauty in her marriage at every season, knowing God is the One who will supply all that she needs for this man, for this marriage, for this moment.

We also want you to be hopeful about your marriage. As we talked with hundreds of women while working on this book, many expressed fears about the approaching empty nest, but those who had already walked through their first couple of years were generally very excited about their marriages. Couples that prepared ahead for the transition have had less marital friction. In fact, many women have said that this is the most fun they've had with their husband in years!

Four things will help you prepare your marriage for the transition.

### 1. Reconfirm Your Covenant

*For better or worse, in sickness and in health, until we are parted by death.*

Most likely you made a promise with these or similar words at your wedding. You may not have understood or appreciated it at the time, but you were establishing a covenant—a solemn vow between two individuals and a holy God that is to last a lifetime. It is not a contract with escape clauses; a covenant is meant to be permanent.

When we first made these promises, we were full of joy and hope and visions of bliss. We didn't know what was ahead, but we knew that this was the person we wanted to spend the rest of our life with. Now, once again, we don't exactly know what the future looks like, but we do know who we want to spend it with.

How the empty nest impacts your marriage is going to be determined to a large extent by how you have nurtured your marriage thus far. If you've focused on your kids exclusively and neglected to nurture your marriage, you will have a harder time.

No matter what you have or haven't done, God can still build a new relationship. No matter what your history, the promises you made to each other before God many years ago are still in effect. This season can be a fresh start; it can even be the best season of your marriage. You can begin by recommitting yourself to your mate.

Friends of ours have a unique way of celebrating their anniversary. Each year on the exact date of their wedding, they travel to a new state and reenact their vows. They try to engage a local pastor to officiate at this special ceremony. Their goal is to do this in a different state each year—and we hope they run out of states before they run out of years!

While we might not be able to travel as they can, we can learn from their example of frequently and creatively celebrating their marriage covenant.

As you approach the empty nest, plan a specific way to celebrate this new season in your life as a couple and to recommit your lives to each other. Make it special and meaningful. Just as your marriage began with a celebration, this new season of your marriage will benefit from a renewal of your vow "till death do us part."

### 2. Discuss Your Expectations

A dad was helping his daughter pack boxes in anticipation of her leaving for college. Not only was she unusually close to her parents, but she was also the last child to leave. Looking up at her dad, she asked with real concern in her voice, "Dad, what's it gonna be like when I'm gone?"

Without missing a beat he replied, "It's going to be clothing optional in every room!"

This husband definitely had his own picture of what *his* empty nest should look like!

Chances are you've thought about your expectations more than your husband has. Several friends on the verge of the empty nest were discussing their expectations. One commented, "My husband is needy. I'm afraid I'll become engulfed in his neediness."

Another chimed in, "My husband is completely independent. I'm afraid that without the glue of the kids, we'll drift apart."

One friend wanted to discuss sex: "My husband has big visions of sexual intimacy. I don't know if I can handle his expectations!"

Some men may expect their wives to be like their mothers were in their season of the empty nest. Our mothers were more likely to turn their attentions more fully to their husbands, serving them in fresh ways rather than seeking their own interests. Yet today's women are more career oriented, more independent. Neither is better. We are merely the products of different times. But our expectations will be shaped in part by the homes in which we were raised. It's helpful to recognize this and factor it in.

Expectations can be boundless, and many times you'll discover that your expectations do not become reality. Sheila's husband was afraid that she'd take all of her attention and focus it on him. But their nest wasn't empty very long before he felt Sheila was too busy for him!

It will be most helpful if the two of you begin to discuss the empty nest *before* you actually get there. Joe and Pam have begun to do this. A busy pediatrician, Joe has always been a highly involved dad. He and Pam have raised six kids, and even though their youngest has a couple of years left at home, they are already discussing what life will be like when she leaves. Joe wonders how he can cut back at the office in order to spend more time with Pam. He also longs for a new venture in which they can make a difference together in the lives of others. He and Pam don't know yet what this new season will look like, but in talking about it now, they are beginning to form common expectations and goals for their next great adventure. Simply talking is adding glue to their relationship.

Set aside a time to discuss this new season. Share how each of you is feeling about what lies ahead. And don't be surprised if he hasn't thought about it at all!

### 3. Plan for Fun

It's easy to fall into the trap of taking ourselves too seriously. There are so many demands that some days we feel like just getting through is about all we can handle. Many of us have forgotten how to have fun. Because we are so busy, fun gets relegated to vacations. Our daily lives become measured by how much we accomplish; we're servants to our to-do lists. We're happy if we can check things off, and moody if we don't. Both of us have experienced this, and both of us are trying to learn how to inject more fun into our daily lives, particularly with our husbands.

Because life is so often serious, we are finding that we have to work at laughing and having fun. We are also discovering that the advent of the empty nest provides a great opportunity to discover new ways of having fun as a couple. And they don't have to be big things. It's not really the big things—vacations, trips, etc.—that make a difference in relationships. More often it's the little things that transform.

Sometimes it's the spontaneous things.

BARBARA: Dennis and I decided we would take turns once a month planning a fun event. This would ensure that twice a month we did something lighthearted. Once I planned a coffee date at a local bookstore during which we looked at home decorating books and travel magazines and simply dreamed.

We also realized that one of the blessings of the empty nest was that we could do things on the spur of the moment. With kids, we'd been "responsible" for so long that we had to relearn how to be spontaneous.

One warm Sunday in January as Dennis and I were leaving church, we realized that we didn't *have* to do anything. So on the spur of the moment we decided to go on a picnic! Since we had no food in the fridge at home, we stopped at the store, and what we bought wasn't nutritious! Simply eating what we really liked, atop a trailside rock in the woods, made us feel like teenagers again. It was a wonderful respite from the demands of life to spend the afternoon leisurely hiking and picnicking.

We asked some friends what they were doing to infuse their marriages with fun. Here are some ideas they shared:

- Beth and Derek began to go for an early morning jog together. Another couple began walking after work. For both couples, these times provided an opportunity to talk without being interrupted. (Hint: Learn to ask questions that call for more than one-word answers.)

- Ann and her husband love good food. As they entered the empty nest, they decided to take turns choosing a new restaurant to go to each week. Pretending to be food critics, they evaluated their meal and worked up a list of recommendations for their friends.

- Vicki and her husband, Tom, along with two other couples, decided to take a Spanish class together. They're enjoying one another's company while taking on the challenge of learning something new.

- Judy's nest is empty and her husband, Sam, has retired. With completely new schedules, they realized they could make time to study the Bible together. Since both are early risers, they began to have coffee together. One reads the Bible passage from a daily study guide, and then they discuss the written questions. They keep a commentary by their kitchen table and have fun delving into its observations. As a part of their study, they pray for each other's concerns, for their kids and grandkids, and for other people and issues.

Another way to have fun is to rekindle the romance in your marriage. Now that the kids are gone, spontaneity can return to this area of your marriage, too. But expectations will need to be discussed, and both of you need to realize that creative lovemaking may need to be relearned.

One husband suggested to his wife, "I think we should have gourmet cooking nights, and you should wear one of those topless aprons." She thought that was a little weird for her, but she did get the message that her husband was longing for some fun and playfulness in their lovemaking.

Likewise, if you need to add some playfulness, grab a blanket, candles, and special beverages and make love in a different room in your house. Find an empty field and just lie there together on a blanket and enjoy the peace and quiet. As a woman, it's important that you never underestimate the power of initiating sex with your husband. Even if you are tired and don't feel like it, you honor him by initiating sex from time to time. His identity as a man is strongly tied to the physical act.

On the other hand, you may find that you are more interested in sex than he is. A physician friend shared with us that he includes a sexual intimacy questionnaire as part of his history on adults during their annual exams. Much to his surprise, for couples in their forties and older, wives answer three to one over husbands that they desire sexual intercourse more often. In midlife a man's sexual appetite often decreases. Frequently, a good physical will reveal something that can be treated. By all means seek competent medical advice. This part of your relationship is too important to ignore.

One of the benefits of having fun together is that you will naturally have more time to talk and to dream about your future. As you ride in your car for a day trip to the beach, hike through the woods, or just walk in your neighborhood, conversation will begin spontaneously—slowly perhaps, but it will happen. What are your expectations? What are your husband's? You may be surprised at what he says.

### 4. Dream About a New Mission Together

Taking time as a couple to focus on one another is crucial to our sense of well-being and important for a vital marriage. Yet it isn't enough. Our ultimate focus is to be on others rather than on ourselves. This is the second part of the Great Commandment (see Matthew 22:37–39) and also the key to joy. Now is the time to consider the question *What is God calling us to do together that will make a positive difference in the lives of others?*

Jane and Don have raised four kids; they have always loved young people. As empty nesters, they decided to invite several young couples into a fellowship group with the purpose of mentoring them in growing strong families. Each couple read the same book on this topic, and they discussed what they had read. It was a safe place for these young couples to ask questions. Jane and Don had "been there." They didn't feel like experts (does anyone?), but they did understand. Most of all Jane and Don *loved* these couples. Because of their willingness to give their time and their hearts, they are having an impact on the next two generations.

Jeff and Ellie have spent years in Alcoholics Anonymous and Al-Anon. Through their own experiences they have realized how hard it is for those in recovery to find friends. Many have had to break ties with their old crowd, and as a result they need new friends. As a couple, Jeff and Ellie have begun to initiate social outings with some of these couples who are longing for someone to walk alongside them during this difficult period.

Bill, a businessman, has begun to use his skills in training ministry leaders in ways of management. Because his wife has been involved in ministry for years, she has a keen sense of what is needed, and their combined backgrounds are complementing each other to meet the needs of others.

Some couples find it helpful at this stage to draft a vision statement for their marriage. (We'll talk more about this in chapter 11.) The exercise of drafting this statement can be helpful if for no other reason than to give a couple the opportunity to talk about their hopes, dreams, and expectations. More important, a vision statement helps a husband and wife think about a purpose that they can pursue *together*. One friend told us, "In a way we've lived separate lives as my husband has focused on work and I've focused on family. Simply by talking about a vision statement, I realized we were beginning to think as *we* now rather than *you* and *I*. That was encouraging."

There is no limit to the new ventures that are available to empty-nest couples; and in planning for and pursuing these ventures together, your marriage can thrive. Ask God to give you wisdom and watch Him work in ways that will go beyond your plans and even your dreams.

> Now to Him who is able to *do immeasurably more* than all we ask or imagine, according to his power that is at work within us, to him be glory in the church and in Christ Jesus throughout all generations, for ever and ever!
>
> Ephesians 3:20–21 NIV (emphasis ours)

## Take the Next Step

· · · · ·

1. Make a list of what you most admire or appreciate about your husband. Express those things to him.

2. What are potential areas of conflict or challenges that you might face in the future? What can you do to prepare for them in a positive manner?

3. Set aside a date to begin discussing your expectations of each other in this new season. Also, plan for some times of fun for just the two of you. And if you are highly motivated, begin to talk together about your vision for the future and what mission you might want to work on as a couple.

## Recommended Reading

*Letters to My Daughters: The Art of Being a Wife* by Barbara Rainey (Bethany House, 2016)

*A Celebration of Sex After 50* by Douglas E. Rosenau, James K. Childerston, Carolyn Childerston (Thomas Nelson, 2004)

*Fight Fair!: Winning at Conflict Without Losing at Love* by Tim and Joy Downs (Moody, 2010)

*Rekindling the Romance: Loving the Love of Your Life* by Dennis and Barbara Rainey with Bob DeMoss (Thomas Nelson, 2004)

# Maggie's Story

## Giving Back

"I've always been happiest when all my 'chicks' are in the nest," Maggie reflected. "Since we struggled with infertility for years, I was especially thrilled when we had our two girls. I loved my years of being Mom, and it was a heart-wrenching moment as we drove off the college campus with our youngest in the rearview mirror."

About the time her nest was emptying, Maggie's husband, Dave, was considering retiring from his job as a policeman. Even with such a stressful job, his priority had always been Maggie and the girls. When Maggie and Dave were first married, they walked into a couples' class at their church. They were young and teachable and desperately wanted to build a strong marriage and close-knit family. The teaching and mentoring they received from older couples had a huge impact on their own priorities as they raised their family.

Maggie had prayed early in their marriage for a ministry she and Dave would share. God answered that prayer, and for twenty-five years they have served together, behind the scenes, at Weekend to Remember conferences around the country.[2] Furthermore, with their heart for couples, God also blessed them with the opportunity to teach a young-marrieds Sunday school class for several years.

But Maggie had a second prayer request.

> I knew that I wanted to do some things with my husband, but I also needed to have something of my own. I began to pray that God would give me a personal ministry.
>
> Over the years I had observed some wives who lived only in the shadows of their husbands. They hadn't pursued their own ministry, passions, or interests—it was as if these wives had no identity of their own. I did not want to be like that.

Again God provided. Maggie's personal ministry took on several forms throughout the years prior to their empty nest. But once the chicks were gone from the nest, she was able to devote more time to working with young moms and families.

Since Maggie knew for a decade in advance that she was approaching her double transition of the empty nest and her husband's retirement, she intentionally planned ahead, recognizing that her life experiences had prepared her for the ministries God had for the empty-nest years. She'd seen so much sadness in family relationships that resulted from poor choices, and she longed to help younger women avoid those issues. She and Dave had been on the receiving end of wisdom from older mentors. Now it seemed natural to give back.

Another piece of Maggie's background was the positive experience she'd had homeschooling the girls. It had been a rewarding experience for their family. At the same time, she knew that with the pressures of homeschooling, it was easy to let one's marriage slide. She longed to be able to help young mothers lead balanced lives. It was no surprise when Maggie's passions led her to become codirector of a homeschool support organization.

Another passion Maggie discovered was motivating young women to invest in their marriages and their parenting. She does this now as an occasional speaker for groups such as MOPS (Mothers of Preschoolers). Still, her most precious time is spent with her husband, children, and grandchildren, and in caring for her elderly mother.

Maggie knows that it's helpful to ask several questions as we consider what we should be doing: *What are my core values, and how do they affect my choices? How has God used me in the past? How will He use that in my future? Am I overinvolved in something that is keeping me from a higher calling? Is there something I need to toss that should not be in my life at this particular season?*

And as the seasons of life change, she encourages us to appreciate the routine of the day-to-day, where life happens and where character is formed. "Too often we focus more on the big events of life and consider routine days as unimportant. We must not think of any day as ordinary but live each day fully in the moment, enjoying each season. We can prepare for the future, but we can only live in the moment."

# Chapter 6

## How Do I Relate to My Adult Kids Now?

I saw the angel in the marble and carved until I set him free.

Michelangelo

"Ready. . . . Set. . . . Go!"

It's the simple call to start a race. But it isn't so simple when "Go!" means you're sending your last child off.

Is your child really *ready*? Perhaps some days he's champing at the bit, and other days you glimpse a little fear and anxiety, perhaps masked in a forced bravado. But a mother can tell the difference. Is he *set*? That's hard to know. You've tried to plan for every contingency, but there are too many unknowns waiting out there.

Now it's finally time to *go*. Who would have ever thought a simple two-letter word could evoke so many strong feelings?

Your child's heart is churning with emotions, some realized and some buried for the moment. And what about you? You likely vacillate between being ready for him to leave and shedding tears because you don't want him to go. And those fears—*Is he prepared to handle whatever comes his way? Will he stand strong in his faith or be swayed by the social pressures and skeptical thinkers around him? Have I prepared him adequately?* The what-ifs are haunting.

But there's joy as well—he's excited, and you're excited for him! A great adventure of self-discovery awaits him. You've done the best you could, and now it's time to release him and trust God in his life.

Not so easy, especially the "trusting God in his life" part. In the past when you've trusted God, you've been there to oversee. Now you won't, and it'll be harder to trust because you can't know everything that's going on. You, the mother, are about to experience a deeper meaning of the word *trust*. And that will be good for you.

### Challenges As Our Parenting Roles Change

For some the empty nest begins when the first child leaves home; for others, when the last one gets married. Whenever it begins, the empty nest signals a change in the ways we relate to our children. Many of us will experience three challenges as our parenting roles change.

### *1. The Challenge of Relinquishing Control*

Picture a seesaw. Perhaps you played on one when you were a child. You and a friend would arrange yourselves on the seesaw so as to balance in midair with your feet off the ground. Accomplishing this meant that the heavier child had to move in on one end while the lighter moved out on the other. Both of you had to do some shifting in order to achieve balance.

Relinquishing control involves identifying where you are and then shifting to where you need to be for the sake of your child, your husband, and yourself.

When we talk about relinquishing control, we realize that most of us will fall loosely into one of two categories: the helicopter parent or the hands-off parent.

A helicopter parent is one who hovers over her child. She (or her husband) tends to overparent by trying to micromanage the child's life. Daily phone calls—sometimes several calls a day—are routine. Checking in to see if he got to class on time; if she purchased what she needed—and helping decide what that is; advising on weekend plans, etc. And sometimes the child calls, upset because someone hurt her feelings or he didn't get a class, and they dump their feelings on Mom. They hang up, and Mom's day is ruined because her child is unhappy and she can't fix it.

What we often fail to realize is that, in those situations, we are just the dumping ground. Ten minutes later the child is fine. He or she has moved on, but we are left carrying the burden. "Fix it" personality types are more likely to have a hard time letting go. Why?

There may be a long-established pattern of overinvolvement in the child's life. Mom is used to his dependence upon her, and he is used to being dependent. In some ways a codependent relationship has persisted into his adulthood. In addition, the parent has a *need to be needed*. With the child gone, many of his daily needs vanish, yet Mom unconsciously tries to hold on to being needed.

A helicopter parent genuinely loves her child. She is a good parent. She wants her child to be secure, to feel supported. She wants a deepening friendship. She wants to raise a confident child.

However, by being too involved in her child's life, she is actually undermining these very goals. Instead of the child growing in confidence, her meddling is actually giving the message "You can't cope. You need me to intervene. You don't have the maturity to handle this." This hovering will erode a child's self-confidence rather than build it.

This is also bad for the child, because he or she needs to learn to go more to God for guidance and less to Mom or Dad. Parents don't have all the answers. They won't always be there for their children. But God will.

Our friend Molly offers this advice, which was given to her as she struggled to let go of her son:

A boy who begins to make the transition to manhood needs testing to develop his own confidence. If you enable him too much, he feels weak, as if he believes that you do not have confidence in his ability to do it himself. If you encourage him and model to him that he "can do all things through Christ who strengthens [him]" (Philippians 4:13 NKJV), he will turn to Jesus as his true source of strength, not you or even himself. Your job is to pray for him as he steps out in faith.

If our children get the message from us that we are unhappy because they have left, they can begin to feel responsible for our happiness. Of course we miss them, but there is a difference between missing and misery. God did not intend for your child to have that much control over you. You are saddling that child with a burden that should not be his.

What can we do to bring balance, to "hover" less?

- Resist the urge to call or text every day, and don't overreact to your child's calls or texts.
- Say, "I have confidence in you. I *know* you can figure this out." Then let him. A healthy relationship steadily gives decision-making over to the child. Of course, as we saw in chapter 4, there are no guarantees that he will make the right decisions. But for your sake and his, you have to let go.
- Encourage her to pursue God (find a church, a fellowship, a small group).
- Let him know that you are okay, that you are looking forward to this new season and are excited about your future. He needs you to "get a life" because he knows that the more you do, the less you'll meddle in his life.
- Tell her that you and her dad are glad to have time alone together. It gives her a sense of security to know her parents love each other.
- Begin to pursue your next calling. (We'll talk about this in more detail beginning in chapter 9.)

You may not be a helicopter parent who hovers. Perhaps you even occupy the opposite seat on the seesaw as a hands-off parent.

A hands-off parent is not likely to know what her child is up to. She may not have talked to her child in several days or even weeks. She isn't certain what the child's schedule is and figures that no news is good news. This parent is determined not to interfere. She wants the child to make his own decisions.

Why do hands-off parents respond this way? They genuinely believe they have done all they can. They have raised their children to be independent, and now they are on their own. Make no mistake, they love their children just as much as helicopter parents do, but they do not want to hover. They want their children to experience complete freedom so they can develop into healthy adults.

But there's a danger here, too. Independence is healthiest when attained gradually rather than with an instantaneous "Whoopee! I'm free! Now I can do whatever I'd like." Parents need to stay involved in their children's lives; otherwise these newly adult children can feel cut off, set adrift. There may be issues that demand a parent's intervention—an eating disorder, failure to attend classes, severe depression. Every child needs to know they are still on their parents' minds. The absence of communication is not a good or healthy thing. Children need to hear from *both* parents. So what can we do to bring balance to the hands-off approach?

- Call regularly (once a week) simply to check in and find out what's going on in his life.
- Send periodic emails, texts, or handwritten notes of encouragement simply to say, "I'm thinking of you."
- Have the understanding that you will be consulted about major decisions—financial (you are likely contributing to her support, and this assumes accountability), health, safety, a change in housing—especially during her first year away from home.
- Visit during his first year and get to know his friends.

- Learn her weekly schedule so you can pray for her. (It's good to share yours with her so she can pray for you, too.)

Ask yourself, *Which end of the seesaw do I gravitate toward—the helicopter/hovering side, or the hands-off side? What about my husband? What steps do we need to take to balance one another? Or if we are both too heavy on one side, how can we adjust?*

Keep in mind that this is a weaning period for you and your son or daughter, and it will be awkward for a while. At this season you are moving from being a coach to becoming a cheerleader. You are no longer calling every play. Instead, cheer for your children as they succeed and stand by them in comfort when they fail. Your goal is to raise secure, confident kids who have the assurance that as they turn to God, they can be steadfast in whatever life has for them. This happens gradually.

### 2. The Challenge of Letting Them Make Mistakes

Most kids have a rough first year or first semester away from home. For those who go to work full-time, learning that an eight-hour day is normal, that skipping work is not acceptable, and that even dream jobs have boring parts can be a rude awakening.

A college freshman will likely become homesick, lonely, and confused during his first semester. Once the novelty wears off, school work settles in, and relationships become tricky, you may get a phone call about dropping out or transferring.

How do you respond to children who are miserable? Validate their feelings. "I've been there, too. I know it's hard." But then say, "I know this is hard, but you can do it. I have the confidence that you can walk through this difficult time, and I am so proud of you. You are learning valuable lessons and you will be fine. I am praying for you and loving you."

There's an important principle here. Feelings are real. Validate them. But in considering your child's next step, remember that *a mature person makes decisions based on what is right, not on how he feels.*

Do not let them drop out. Do not offer to go get them. Don't bail them out. Something much more important is going on here—character building. They are learning the value of endurance. (In extreme situations, you may need to bring them home or allow them to transfer. But before you do, seek counsel. Be as sure as you can that it is the right thing to do.) Project ten years forward to when this child is in a tough marriage. It hurts. It's hard. But they decide to get help, to stick it out, and to go the distance. Why? Because they learned in their early years the value of endurance.

It's important that we communicate clearly our expectations to our children. Lisa recognized the value of this when her daughter began skipping classes in a particular course during her junior year in college. Although the child knew attendance was required, she didn't think it really mattered as long as she did the work. And she did all the work. But at the end of the semester, she received a failing grade because—you guessed it—she had cut too many classes. Her parents had warned her, and her professor had clearly stated the attendance requirements. She had ignored them, and now she was in a mess. Would she be able to graduate on time? Her parents had been clear in their expectations. They had told her they would pay for four years of college. They ached as they watched her struggle, but they did not intervene.

She met with her professor, did extensive remedial work, and was able to graduate on time. It was a hard but valuable lesson. Their daughter learned that she was not an exception to the rules; they did apply to her. This was great experience for life. It would have been less painful at the time for the parents to have intervened on her behalf. But in the long run, she would not have learned that all actions have consequences. The lessons our kids learn from their mistakes are valuable tools in teaching them how to live.

### 3. The Challenge of Staying Close When They Don't Share Your Faith or Values

As we saw in chapter 4, many of us will struggle with children who have determined to walk away from all that we value. How do we relate to these children, knowing that the direction they are walking is not right—not only morally but also physically or emotionally?

Recently a friend of ours shared that her son had declared to the family that he was gay. She reads his posts on Facebook encouraging others to be brave and come out, and her heart longs to reach his heart. This friend and her husband are in pain. Their precious son they have loved and nurtured has walked away from their teaching and their faith. His choices are affecting not just Mom and Dad but the entire family, especially his younger siblings still at home.

This is the experience of many moms and dads, either before or during the empty nest. And just as Barbara and Dennis wondered what to do when their daughter made choices they knew were unhealthy, so is our friend, and so will many of you.

One step is to begin to learn more about those who identify as gay. Two excellent books are a good place to start: *The Secret Thoughts of an Unlikely Convert* by Rosaria Champagne Butterfield and *Messy Grace* by Caleb Kaltenbach. You can also listen to interviews with these authors, both of whom lived in that world for years, on FamilyLifeToday.com.[1]

You may not be facing the challenge of a son or daughter who has come out as gay, but instead you may watch your newly liberated child fall in love and decide to move in with his or her intended, confidently telling you, "What difference does it make if we plan to get married eventually? And besides, we are saving a lot of money sharing the rent."

Cohabitation is the new marriage preparation of choice. Today approximately 65 percent of all couples choose to live together prior to marriage; roughly 7 million couples are cohabiting.[2] The impact of divorce has convinced many young adults that the risk of marriage is just too great, that living together first is the only way to discover if they want to spend the rest of their lives with each other. A book you might want to read is *The Ring Makes All the Difference*, by Glenn Stanton. The radio interview with this author is also available for download at FamilyLifeToday.com.[3]

So how do you keep a relationship going while you watch your child, whom you love deeply, walk in ways you wouldn't choose? First and always, it is crucial that you give grace and remember that we are all sinners. God doesn't grade on a curve, so your sin needs forgiveness as much as your child's. Humble yourself first. If you harbor any judgment in your heart at all, your child will spot it a mile away. This isn't easy, but God is fully able to give you what you absolutely do not have. And that is both a miracle and the kind of heart your children need to see in you first. If you can love them no matter what, then they are more likely to believe God can love them, too.

Second, try to find ways to connect over what you know they love or what you know you have in common.

When Samantha's son was struggling with drugs and alcohol, it was terribly difficult to find common ground. What could they talk about? How could they spend time together? They had so little in common. But there was hockey; they were all big-time ice hockey fans. During a difficult year, the one thing the family could agree on was the pro hockey team in their city. So off to the games they went, as a family. Hockey became a sort of glue that held this family together until they could work through rehab and counseling. It gave them a safe place, a common interest.

It's important to stay connected. Get to know your child's friends even if you don't like them. It's all too easy to make judgments before we even take the time to know them. If your kids see you trying hard to connect with their friends, they will loosen up. And if your interest is genuine, that friend may respond to you, and his response will make an impression on your child.

Staying close does not mean you change your standards. If your college son brings home the girl he is living with, you put them in separate bedrooms. It's your home. And in your home only folks who are married sleep together. But while they are visiting, you do your best to get to know her, to make her feel welcome, to love her. This is grace—unconditional love. And it's at the core of our faith.

Again, we have to remember that demonstrating unconditional love while adhering to absolute truth may be the very thing that draws a wayward child back in.

Relating to our adult kids isn't all about challenges. There's a lot of fun in store, too!

## Connecting With Your Adult Children

New intersections lie ahead. Opportunities are opening up that will enable you to connect with your adult children in fresh ways. In this season, you will see even more clearly the subtle changes that have been taking place in your relationship with your children. As they grow into adulthood, you will find that they are becoming peers. Your friendship with your son or daughter will become similar to the friendships you have with your own siblings. Consider the following ways to connect.

### Share Your New Lives Together

My (Susan's) refrigerator has always been a mess of notes and photos. When the kids were in college, each semester they wrote out their schedules on pieces of paper and stuck them on the refrigerator. It made it easy for me to know what they were doing.

On Mondays, Susy had a tough 8:00 a.m. class; I needed to pray for her. Libby had a sorority meeting on Sunday nights; I was reminded to pray for her new friends. Chris had an article for the school paper due; he needed guidance. These schedules helped me feel in touch even though the kids were away.

This connection should run both ways; share your lives with your kids. When you touch base by phone, let them know what's on your schedule, what you need prayers for. One of the real blessings of writing this book is that many Rainey and Yates kids were praying (and continue to pray) for the two of us. They knew when we were writing, the frustration of blank pages, and they were thrilled when they called and one of us said, "You know the chapter we were stuck on—we got it! Thanks so much for praying!"

Remember the two categories that are helpful in looking for fresh ways to share our lives: schedules and relationships. Each of us has a typical schedule and each of us has relationships. Even your children who aren't living as you'd hoped. It helps conversations continue by asking questions that fall into one of these categories. "Who have you enjoyed spending time with lately? Who would you like to get to know? What's on your schedule this week?" Questions like these help you know what one another's life is like.

Set aside your agenda when your kids come home for a visit. This will enable you to hang out with them. Listen more and advise less. Ask for their input on things, too.

If you have multiple kids, it's important to remember to focus on the child you are with. If you are always talking about one sibling, the others may feel sad, as if you are not interested in them.

You may be having a crisis or a prolonged health issue with one of your children. It is natural to be consumed by the situation of the "needy child," and it's easy to let their needs overtake your family for a long period of time. Take care that you don't neglect a "healthy child." The healthy child still longs for a connection with you, and he or she may feel reticent to say anything because of the sibling's needs. Simply make a priority of spending time alone with each of them in their worlds. Focus on them and resist the tendency to let your concerns for the needy sibling dominate your conversation.

### Foster Sibling Relationships

With our children growing up and going their own ways, we have a fresh longing for them to stay connected to one another. More than anything we desire for them to love Christ and to love each other. Hopefully, we have come through the worst years of sibling rivalry. Now we can be proactive in moving them toward one another.

BARBARA: Not long after our oldest, Ashley, got married, we realized our family times together were changing. Ashley was now alternating holidays with her husband's family, which was the right thing to do, but it meant our kids were not together as often as they used to be. We knew it would only get more complicated with each additional child who got married and moved away.

Taking a cue from a family who was ahead of us in life, Dennis and I began to discuss and plan for an annual family get-together. We knew it would be best to begin before all our kids left home; then it would be a tradition, and no one would want to miss it. The first year was simply a long weekend, but gradually our gathering grew into an entire week.

For several years Dennis and I organized and planned these annual family gatherings, but after ten-plus years, our children's children were getting old enough that they had schedules to be considered. Our grandchildren, as of this writing, now number twenty-three, the oldest of which are involved in a variety of activities—football, gymnastics, camp—during the summer. In addition, none of our six children live in our hometown, so gathering annually requires long car trips for most and plane tickets for two families. The cost of pulling this off became a factor we had to address. At their request, we changed our annual family event to every two years. And even then, not everyone is able to come every time.

I have learned since we first wrote this book that I must give thanks for those who can come and for how long they can stay rather than focus on my loss over those who are absent. Being thankful for what God gives is my new standard.

If having your whole family physically together isn't possible, there are other ways to stay connected. For example, start a family round-robin email; schedule occasional conference calls so everyone can share what's going on in their world; send your high school student to visit his sibling at college; arrange for two of your adult kids to have time together (being in each other's territory without Mom and Dad goes a long way toward bringing siblings together).

SUSAN: When my mom died, she was the last of all four of John's and my parents. It was a very sad time, but it was also a time of thanksgiving for the heritage we had been given. Both sets of parents had shared the same three priorities: faith, family, and serving others. John and I each have three siblings with whom we are very close. Family loyalty has been modeled to us by our parents' generation. Thus, the desire for the Yates kids to be close was natural, given the DNA of both families.

We wanted to do something intentional to help our own children nurture their faith and their relationships with one another. So we decided to take a portion of our small inheritance and designate it as a "legacy fund" in honor of our parents. We told our kids that they could draw from this fund (which we administered) for any conferences, retreats, or classes that would be faith-building and for any trips to be with their siblings.

For many years our adult kids were scattered from England to California, and this fund enabled them to visit each other, to walk in one another's shoes, and to form adult friendships with their siblings. Nothing brings greater joy to a parent than watching their kids love each other.

### Plan a Wedding With Care

Chances are you'll be planning a wedding sometime in the future. It might come just as you are approaching the empty nest. This happened to both of us. And we've learned a few things, especially from our mistakes.

SUSAN: After Allison (my firstborn) got engaged, everyone went into planning mode. Never having done this before, and having heard stories of the tension a wedding brings out, I really wanted it to be a good experience.

I remember going to Allison and saying, "Honey, I'm so excited for you and Will. I want this whole process to be a good one; but I need to tell you that I don't know what I'm doing or how to do this, so if I get too bossy, you'll have to tell me."

This cleared the air, and when I did get too bossy, she told me. I apologized and backed off, and we laughed! A few years later our twin daughters, Susy and Libby, got married six weeks apart. Feeling a bit overwhelmed by all the details and decisions, I prayed again for the process to be fun for everyone. I wrote myself a note and put it on the refrigerator:

> *Remember, Susan, you are not mainly planning*
> *an event; you are building a family, and*
> *relationships are more important than details.*

I was to need this reminder many times over the next several months.

When your children get married, your family priorities will change again and theirs will, too. No longer are your relationships with your children their priority. Their priorities now become their relationships with their spouses. Our role as parents is to help them leave and encourage them to cleave and to become one flesh (see Genesis 2:24).

For a dad, giving his daughter away can be extremely difficult. He is likely to be overwhelmed with conflicting emotions—gratitude for her happiness and for this wonderful moment, but saddened that she's now pledging herself first to another man who's taking over the responsibility of protecting and providing for his little girl. Dad can't help but wonder if the young man will really be a good husband.

On the other hand, giving a son away can be more difficult for the mom. After all, your daughter will still be your friend, but you are about to be replaced by another woman in your son's life. Furthermore, if you're a mother of all sons, you may experience an even deeper grief when your last son marries. Your loss is magnified because you have given all your children away. His wife may not want to be your friend, at least not right away, so your sadness can be acute.

The Yateses have a family tradition of a big rehearsal party the night before the wedding. Friends and family give toasts, present hilarious skits, and honor the couple in a variety of ways. Even though I already loved my future daughter-in-law, I knew that I was about to take a step back, and I needed to be clear about this in my own mind.

I wanted to do something to signify the changing of priorities that was about to take place—something that I could look back to in the future. I decided to write a poem to my future "daughter" to read to her at the party. In it I said that I was now stepping back to become the #2 woman in my son's life, and she was to be #1. To signify this exchange, I gave her a gold necklace with two pendants—a cross to signify Christ as her Savior and a number 1 to signify that she was now the #1 woman in my son's life.

Our role is to help the newly married couple cling to each other. As parents, we can either make that difficult or help to ease the way. When your newlywed child calls to ask, "What couch do you think I should get?" your response should be, "What does your spouse think?"

We should free them from us and push them to each other. It doesn't mean that we can't give advice. It does mean that most often we should wait to be asked. And in all that we say, we must keep in mind the priority of *their* marriage.

To emphasize this priority, both of us have paid for all our married kids to attend a Weekend to Remember marriage conference. Each of Susan's went after being married for at least a year, while Barbara's attended after they became engaged and before they married.

Of her experience, Barbara's daughter Ashley says, "This conference gave Michael and me the opportunity to anticipate some of the issues we would face as a married couple before we faced them. We had good interaction on those topics at the conference. And it gave us a common language for discussing marriage together, which was helpful since we came from very different backgrounds."

All of our kids have benefited. We know this because they've encouraged their friends to attend. This is a great gift you can give to your kids and their friends. We often give this conference as a wedding gift.[4]

### Build a Good Relationship With Your New Son or New Daughter

We hate in-law jokes, especially mother-in-law bashing. Perhaps it's because we are both mothers-in-law, and we so desperately want to be good ones. Oh, we know we fail (we do as moms and wives, too), but we don't think it's helpful to make fun of others. It gives people the mind-set that this relationship has to be difficult, but it doesn't!

Beginning a good relationship with your new son or new daughter happens when you determine not to view them as in-laws but as your kids, period. Barbara sees herself as having twelve children, and Susan sees herself as having ten.

Nurturing this new relationship will take time, and everyone has to be patient. It's not realistic to think you'll feel totally comfortable during the first year. You have to get to know each other.

Study your "new" child. Find out his or her interests, and try to become involved in those interests in some way. If they live close and are into photography, learn about photography. If it seems natural, suggest taking a photography class together. If they live far away, send them notes or emails. Ask your own child, "How can I love your spouse? Please give me advice on how I can show love in the way that is appropriate for them."

Just asking your own child will be a great encouragement. They desperately want their spouse and their parents to like one another. We each have different love languages. Find out what your new children's love languages are and communicate in a way that they will readily receive.

### Nurture Relationships With the Families Your Kids Have Married Into

Not only has our newlywed child just inherited a new family, but we have joined this new family to ours. We need to be intentional about making this a strong merger. Several things will be helpful:

**Remember that your kids are just as much theirs as they are yours.** This can be a hard concept to get our heads and hearts around. For all of your lives these have been *your* kids. Now all of a sudden you have to share them, not just a little, but equally. Sometimes it may not feel equal. In fact, you may be getting shortchanged. Your new daughter may want to spend more time with her own family than with yours. Be patient and give her a few years to adjust. Be grateful and show appreciation every time she makes an effort to be with you.

**Don't compete with the other family.** They may be able to provide more financial help, to plan better vacations, to be more involved in your future grandchildren's lives. The natural inclination will be to compete, but this is truly selfish because it subtly says, "We want to be the ones they like the best." This attitude will only lead to bitterness and friction, and it will ultimately make everyone's lives miserable. Instead, always choose the high road. Never talk badly about your own child's new family. Choose to be content in your own situation and grateful for whatever the other parents can do, be it more than you or less.

**Initiate ways to love your child's new family.** When we (John and Susan) were about to host our last wedding, we decided to have a special party to honor our kids' in-laws. Each of these five sets of parents was an answer to our prayers. While we were raising our own children, John and I prayed specifically for our children's future spouses (should God lead them to marry), and we prayed as well for God to give their parents wisdom and encouragement as they raised them.

We were also hoping there were five sets of parents or grandparents somewhere praying for us as we raised our kids. We needed those prayers.

At our dinner John and I took time to share what we appreciated about each mom and dad and to thank them for the gift of their children.

No matter what the other family is like, they are now *your* family, too. Your job is to look for the good in them, to pray for them, and to seek specific ways to care for them. You are modeling for your kids and future grandkids the power of grace and loyalty.

### Be Intentional in Offering Encouragement

Martin, a former U.S. congressman and past president of the North Carolina Community College system, is the father of two daughters, and he prayed earnestly for years for his girls' future spouses. He dreamed of having a close relationship with these young men. His daughter Ashley married her high-school sweetheart, Trent. He had been raised by a single-parent mom. Trent's dad had left when he was very young. Although his mom did a terrific job raising her three small kids, her heart was saddened by the void in Trent's life. She longed for him to have a father figure.

In the early years of his marriage, Trent, who was in the navy, was deployed on a submarine for nearly three months. Because Martin himself had served in the navy, he knew how lonely Trent was going to be. He loved this new son and wanted to encourage him. For security reasons, no email was allowed, and only seven telegram messages—limited to fifty words each—were allowed over the three-month period at sea.

Thinking back to his own tour of duty in Vietnam, Martin remembered how much the daily letters from his mom had encouraged him. He decided to write Trent eighty-five letters, one for each day at sea, and give them to him to take along and open on the specific date. Martin looked ahead at his own calendar and projected what he'd be doing that particular day and wrote as if it were the actual day. The notes were brief, often just two or three sentences.

> Dear Trent, I'm having a wonderful time with your beautiful wife today. I hope her being with us will help in her adjustments. I don't have to tell you how much she loves and misses you.
>
> Today we went to Durham for a "pig pickin'" for a cousin who's getting married. It wasn't as good as Wilbur's! [a famous barbecue place in North Carolina that the family had enjoyed].

One day Trent opened his note to find a verse from Proverbs: "Trust in the Lord with all your heart and do not lean on your own understanding. In all your ways acknowledge Him, and He will make your paths straight" (3:5–6). To this day, that remains one of Trent's favorite Bible verses.

Of these letters, Trent says,

Martin is the busiest man I have ever known. He was always traveling, meeting with different college presidents, caring for all sorts of people, and yet he took time to write eighty-five separate notes to me. I knew he was praying for me and thinking of me every day even though we were far apart. I appreciate the fact that he gave me something to look forward to every day. There were so many uncertainties on the sub, but I had one certainty every day, Martin's note.

A wise mother wrote to her son in Vietnam every day. One generation later a very busy man took the initiative to write to his son-in-law every day while he was at sea. What do you suppose will happen in the next generation? May each of us be inspired to leave a legacy of love, encouragement, and support with our children and our new sons and daughters.

> "As for me, this is my covenant with them," says the Lord. "My Spirit, who is on you, will not depart from you, and my words that I have put in your mouth will always be on your lips, on the lips of your children and on the lips of their descendants—from this time on and forever."
>
> Isaiah 59:21 NIV

# Take the Next Step

· · · · ·

1. Read the section "The challenge of relinquishing control" (p. 94) aloud together with your husband. Identify which end of the seesaw each of you occupies. What will you do to achieve more balance? Write down two specific steps that each of you will take.

2. During the empty-nest years, when we are letting our children go, our role shifts from one of direct involvement to more intentional prayer support. Yet often there are so many needs, we hardly know where to begin to pray. Take some time to make a page for each child in a notebook. Write down their needs as you observe them in five areas of growth: spiritual, emotional, physical, mental, and social. (For example, a spiritual need might be for a child to find a fellowship group on campus or in the marketplace; an emotional need might be that a child needs one close friend or an older mentor; a physical need might be finding balance in eating and exercise.) Begin to pray through these needs on a regular basis and record how God answers. Discuss this with your husband. If you are single or your husband is reluctant, do this with a friend and pray for one another's kids.

## Recommended Reading

*How to Really Love Your Adult Child: Building a Healthy Relationship in a Changing World* by Gary Chapman and Ross Campbell (Northfield, 2010)

*The Five Love Languages: The Secret to Love That Lasts* by Gary Chapman (Northfield, 2015)

*Messy Grace: How a Pastor With Gay Parents Learned to Love Others Without Sacrificing Conviction* by Caleb Kaltenbach (Waterbrook, 2015)

*The Secret Thoughts of an Unlikely Convert: An English Professor's Journey Into Christian Faith* by Rosaria Champagne Butterfield (Crown and Covenant, 2012)

*The Ring Makes All the Difference: The Hidden Consequences of Cohabitation and the Strong Benefits of Marriage* by Glenn Stanton (Moody, 2011)

# Ann's Story

## You'll Find It Even When You've Not Looking

Ann was really looking forward to her empty nest. Finally she'd be free to dive more deeply into various volunteer causes about which she was passionate. And she wouldn't have to plan her day to be home at 3:30 when school was out!

"My empty nest quickly became a myth," she says with a laugh.

My youngest son came home after his first semester, and my older sons' jobs moved them back closer to us. I felt like I was running a bed-and-breakfast for my sons and their friends.

Was I disappointed? Perhaps a little, but I was also grateful to have them around. On the one hand, I knew that for my sake I needed to continue to discover where God would have me focus in this new season of life. On the other hand, I wasn't really looking. In fact, I don't think I had a huge need to do something significant. I liked being at home, baking cookies, and taking care of the house.

For years my husband and I had been involved in several internships for college graduates with the purpose of training them to be Christ's representatives in the marketplace. William Wilberforce was our hero, and his life's work to abolish slavery inspired us.

While I was readjusting to my not-so-empty nest, a friend phoned to ask me to meet with a woman who was exploring questions about faith. When I met with this woman, I was impressed by her hunger to know God personally and by her background in working to end slave trafficking. As we got to know one another, her faith became solidified and my heart was touched to support her in her mission.

What simply began as a favor started Ann on the path to discover her next great adventure.

Ann and her new friend began to pray and brainstorm about how they could make a small difference in a huge need. Others came alongside, and the two new friends with an all-volunteer team sponsored a conference to raise awareness of this problem. Then the diplomatic community got involved. Educational groups began to spring up across our country. Their hope is to bring together leaders in various locations and equip them with the tools to discover where and how slave trafficking is happening in their own location and how to help stop it. (An estimated "21 million are enslaved worldwide, generating $150 billion each year in illicit profits for traffickers."[5] This includes child sex slaves and brothels with women and children—all of which can be found in the U.S. and throughout the world.)

In considering how her life has changed, Ann says,

> Looking back at my life, I see threads of interest and seeds of passion that didn't make sense then. Now I see God's hand was in those early circumstances. I knew that one of my gifts was to get behind someone and support them. Even though I didn't intentionally seek out an empty-nest adventure, God knew I was ripe for one, and He dumped one in my lap. My life feels a bit like a tapestry that God has been weaving all along, even though I couldn't see the design in process. Now the design is becoming clearer and its richness amazes me.

# Chapter 7

## How Do I Care for My Extended Family?

To us, family means putting your arms around each other and being there.

Barbara Bush

SUSAN: My life was about to change.

John and I were just getting into bed after a very long day when our phone rang. There was no way I could have prepared for what was to come. It was my mom on the other end of the line. "Susan," she said in a shaky voice. "We've just lost your daddy."

*It can't be!* my heart screamed. Daddy was only seventy-three and the picture of health. But it *was* true. He had been watching basketball with my brother when he collapsed due to an aneurysm and died instantly.

The rest of that night was a blur. We had to track down our kids who were out of town on summer projects, make travel arrangements, and get home as soon as possible. I don't think it really hit me until I walked into my parents' living room a day later and my three siblings burst into tears. The whole thing felt unreal.

Over the next week many people from my parents' church cared for us. All fifteen grandchildren flew in from all over the country for the funeral. Dad had been a man with deep faith, so we had the sweet assurance that he was in heaven. We rejoiced that one day we'd be reunited with him. In the midst of her own pain, Mom was a tower of strength. She busied herself trying to comfort us. Before we had to leave to fly home, Mom pulled me into her arms.

"Susan," she said, "I want you to know one thing for sure. Your daddy knew how much you loved him. He absolutely knew."

Her words brought me great comfort as I walked through my grief in the following months.

What I came to see was that Mom had given me the assurance that I had no regrets in my relationship with Dad. Of course, I wish I could have told him once more, "I love you"; could have apologized yet again for how hard I, a strong-willed child, was to raise; could have snuggled in his arms once more. But I had been given a great gift—a gift of no regrets—because Mom had reminded me, "He knew!"

Ever since my dad's death, I have sought to live in all of my relationships with no regrets. Why? Because we never know when God will call someone home. We don't know when a sibling, a parent, a child, or we ourselves will die. And when that happens, we don't want remorse to pollute our memories.

No, this doesn't mean we have good relationships with everyone. It doesn't mean everyone likes us or agrees with us. It doesn't mean we don't hurt others or aren't wounded by them. But as the apostle Paul said in his letter to the Romans, "If possible, so far as it depends on you, be at peace with all men" (Romans 12:18).

We feel it is important, especially at this season of life, to approach our relationships intentionally with no regrets.

What does this look like?

Our friend Carleen remarked that one of the surprises for her during this empty-nest season is the new way she is connecting with her mother.

I never did like my mother very much. However, when our last child left, I determined to spend more time with her. I don't want to look back one day and have regrets about my relationship with my mom. She lives in the same town that I do, so I've begun to go over to her house more, to go shopping with her, and to go out to lunch. In fact, I am discovering how much I like her! Now I'm getting to know her as my friend, and this is helping me feel less anxious about the tension between my middle child and me. I have hope that one day even she and I will be friends!

BARBARA: When my nest was finally empty, I made a renewed effort to visit my parents, who lived two hours away, once a month. Though I didn't always make it every month, the goal helped me plan to make the drive to see them more often than if I'd not had a goal at all. In 2012 my father died at the age of ninety, and I was so grateful I'd made seeing both my parents regularly a priority. As Susan mentioned, it's a wonderful feeling to have no regrets.

Now that it's just my mother, my goal is the same: see her once a month if possible and call several times a week. With no children at home tying me to school and schedules that weren't under my control, you would think the goal of seeing my parents, and now my mom, would be easy, but I still find that I have to make a decision on when I can go each month and put it on my calendar. Otherwise, something that seems urgent will crowd this time out.

### Trading Places

Just as many of us hit the empty nest, we are also grappling with the issues of caring for elderly—and possibly ill—parents, and losing our parents. A newscast once featured a special on caring for elderly parents. It was called "Trading Places." In a sense that's part of what we do in this season—trade places with our parents by "parenting" them. Caring for parents is an increasingly common responsibility for empty nesters. A Pew Research Center study reports, "Among all adults with at least one parent age 65 or older,

30% say their parent or parents need help to handle their affairs or care for themselves."[1]

When we married, we not only got new husbands, we got new families. And our husbands did, too! Of course, as newlyweds we had no clue how these relationships would develop. Fast-forward several years to the present: With our kids now leaving home, we have a new opportunity to kindle the relationship with both sets of parents. (Remember the commandment "Honor your father and your mother, so that you may live long in the land the Lord your God is giving you" Exodus 20:12 NIV.)

Some have painful memories and estranged relationships with parents or in-laws, while others are lovingly bonded. Whatever your history or pattern of relating has been, why not take advantage of the opportunity this season gives—a fresh start with your parents? And again we emphasize: It's not *my parents* or *his parents*. They are both *yours together*. Shifting to this mind-set will help you avoid some marital conflict and encourage you to love each other's parents intentionally.

Let's face it: It will be our turn soon. Not too many years from now, our kids will be doing for us what we are doing for our parents. It's to our advantage to set a good example!

Where to begin? How should we care for our parents in this season of life?

### Initiate Activities and Show Thoughtfulness

**Write to them.** With the convenience of email, handwriting has been virtually set aside, yet there's something special about receiving a personal note or letter. Take time to write to your parents—both sets. Thank them for what they did right—for bringing you and your spouse into the world, for getting up when you were sick, for specific strengths you have appreciated that they instilled in you, for the things you appreciate that you haven't thanked them for. As you consider writing a note, a letter, or even a tribute to your parents and in-laws, you might find it helpful to read the book *The*

*Forgotten Commandment: Experiencing the Power of Honoring Your Parents*, which explains how to write a memorable letter of honor and gratitude they will truly cherish.

Since we've walked through the parenting years ourselves, we should have a better appreciation for what our parents went through. They may have done many things wrong. We have, too. But now we have the gift of perspective that we didn't have in the early years. It would be easy for us to focus on the mistakes our parents made, but it's much better to focus on what they did right. After all, we hope our adult kids will choose to focus on what we have done right rather than on our many mistakes.

What better gift could you give?

**Phone them.** About a year before my dad died, Dennis and I (Barbara) called to wish my parents a happy anniversary. Mom was at the grocery store, so Dad answered the phone. A World War II veteran, he never showed much emotion or need for people. All my life he frowned on phone calls—when made purely for visiting—considering them frivolous. He was a man of few words. His belief was to say what you want and hang up. In his last few years, however, he began to talk a little more, and every time I called he said, "Thank you for calling."

On this occasion I told him why we called, and then Dennis took the phone and asked my dad how he achieved perfection in marriage in their fifty-nine years together. It made my dad laugh, which was delightful to hear. When I got the phone back, he said again how much he appreciated our calling. I heard real gratitude in his voice. Though conversations with him were still brief, it was encouraging to know my calls were meaningful to him.

Now that some of us are in-laws ourselves, we know how much it means when a child's spouse calls simply to say, "I was just thinking about you and wanted to see how you are doing." It means the world.

When we were young, we didn't realize that older people had many of the same needs we did. We assumed they had outgrown those things. But as we ourselves get older, it becomes clearer to us that we really aren't all that different from our twenty-five-year-old. We still want to be loved, to be appreciated. We wonder if we are pleasing our parents. We so badly want to. In many ways we are merely little girls in antique bodies. So are our mothers.

**Visit them.** With the kids gone, we may have more time for our parents. Weekends are freer, making it possible to visit our out-of-town parents more often. We have to make it a priority and put it on the calendar. Schedules will quickly fill up. If we simply assume we'll go see them as time allows, it probably won't happen. Even if our parents live close by, it's easy to become so involved in other things that we hardly take time to visit them. We don't want to regret one day that we didn't make the time to be with them.

**Forgive them.** *What if we are estranged? What if we have wounds from our past that have not healed? What if . . . ?* The cross is the keystone of the Christian faith. It speaks forgiveness. Shouts it, actually.

No matter what our parents did or didn't do, we can choose to forgive. The failure to forgive will lead to a life marked by bitterness, and bitterness does not lie dormant. It festers and grows. Even if a parent has not repented, even if the wounds are deep, the pain still fresh—even then, with God's help—we can forgive. God's healing will begin as we choose by faith (not feelings) to forgive. No parent sets out to do a bad job of raising their kids. Often our parents did the best they could, given their background and upbringing. For some of us, leaving a strong legacy to our children will begin by our taking steps to forgive our parents.

On the other hand, we may be in the position of needing to ask for forgiveness. Perhaps we have not honored our parents in the way we should. We may need to go to them, admit our shortcomings, and seek their forgiveness.

Perhaps you feel it's too late. It isn't! It's never too late to do what is right. Write the letter, make the call, go visit. God can redeem any relationship.

### Care for Them in Their Latter Years

Healthy parents, single parents, incapacitated parents, estranged parents. No matter what situation we face, here are some guiding principles that can be helpful:

**Assess their situation.** What are your parents' needs at the moment, and what does the future look like? Where do you live in relationship to them? Will you need to move them closer to you? Will they need to one day move in with you? What family support is available? What resources (e.g., financial, health care, housing, etc.) are available?

It is important to communicate clearly with your siblings, if you have them, as you make decisions about your aging parents. Working together to solve problems could become an opportunity for you to deepen your family relationships.

**Prepare yourself to make hard decisions about their care.** Encourage your parents to make their own choices as long as they can, but realize that the time may come when you'll need to step in. You must be willing to decide what is medically and practically best for them even if they don't agree. They may think they can still drive a car or live alone when they truly cannot. You may have to intervene for their safety and the safety of others. Don't be surprised if they resist some of your decisions.

It's sometimes helpful to call a family conference with your siblings to discuss your parents' needs and the options for their care. Be willing to do research to determine what help is available. Then present some simple options from which your parents can choose. Simplifying complex issues into manageable options helps in dealing with the elderly.

**Make sure their affairs are in order.** Many times a parent becomes incapacitated or dies with little or no instructions, an unclear will, and no guidance for those left behind. Often this lack of planning will cause endless hours of work on the part of their children and may even cause friction between family members as to how things should be handled. These situations can be avoided. Simple planning

121

can prevent many problems and alleviate the chance of disagreement. (We have included a helpful checklist in appendix 1.) Take some time during the empty-nest years to help your parents make sure their affairs are in order. This is a good time to get your *own* things in order, too. You will be doing your children a great service.

**Be willing to make sacrifices.** A year after her dad died, Peggy and her husband decided they should move Peggy's mother into their home. It was a huge decision for them and their three children. There were many wonderful, precious times during those years, but other times Peggy cried out to the Lord, "I don't think I can do this!" And she always sensed Him say, "Yes, you can. I will help you."

Eighteen years later, on a sunny afternoon, Peggy's mom looked deep into her eyes and said, "Thank you for taking such good care of me." Early the next morning she had a massive stroke and never recovered.

Peggy still cherishes that final blessing. Even more, she is thankful to God that through caring for her mother, she experienced His work in her life and in the lives of her children in remarkable ways.

We won't all have an elderly parent move in with us. For a variety of reasons, this is not always the best solution. But each of us must be willing to make sacrifices to be able to care for our parents. Peggy's word for us is this: God will equip us to do whatever He asks of us.

**Pray for them.** For years Audrey prayed for her mother to come to faith in Christ. She shared her own faith journey with her mom, and even though they lived an ocean apart, she visited her as often as possible. At eighty-six, her mom's health began to fail. Rushing to her side Audrey pleaded, "Lord, please help Mummy come to know you and let me be with her when she dies."

Even as she prayed, Audrey wondered if it was too late. Her mom had never been interested in matters of faith. But Audrey was in for a surprise, as her mom asked if it was too late for her to receive communion in the church service at her retirement home.

Audrey said, "Why, Mummy, it's never too late!" and she arranged for a minister to come and explain the message of Christ to her mom and to prepare her for communion. Through his gentle explanation her eyes were opened with a new understanding of the deity of Christ and of His promise of eternal life. Three months later, as Audrey sat on the bed holding her, Mummy quietly slipped away. Overwhelmed, Audrey whispered, "Oh, God, you have given me more than I could ask or imagine. It wasn't too late for Mummy."

**Maintain a sense of humor.** When we are dealing with aging, sickness, and dying, life feels heavy. It's a good time to look for the humorous things and to laugh. Often it's the elderly who can help us laugh! They have learned not to take life so seriously. And they can say the funniest things.

Tammy's mother is ninety-eight. For years she has lived with Tammy, whose nursing background enables her to care for her in her home. Recently, however, her mother told Tammy that she was thinking of moving out.

"Why, Mother?" Tammy asked. "Aren't you happy with the care here?"

"It's not the care," her mother responded. "It's just that I'd like to be with some men!"

## Reconnecting With Siblings and Their Families

Meredith is a new empty nester. For several months she was busy getting her last child ready to go off to college. During that time she felt a pull to reconnect with her siblings. Her brother, Ned, was single, in his forties, and had several disabilities. Meredith realized that she needed to be more intentional in connecting with him. When their parents were gone, he would need more assistance from her.

So she arranged for Ned to come from another state for a visit. This took careful planning. She wanted him to feel special and cared for, so she arranged events that he could enjoy. She pointed out to him the things she appreciated about him. She observed that he is very thoughtful and notices what other people like. He brought Meredith a home and garden magazine because he knows she likes gardens. Meredith was quick to say to him, "You are so thoughtful. You have such a kind heart."

123

An unexpected blessing came for Meredith as she watched her eighteen-year-old son care for his uncle.

"We went for a boat ride, and my son offered his hand when Ned became unsteady. He hung out with him and included him in his activities. My brother elicited compassion and thoughtfulness in my son that I don't always see!"

BARBARA: Several years ago, my sister-in-law was diagnosed with breast cancer. At that time I still had four children at home, plus two just beginning college. I remember praying for Donna and being concerned for her, but I did not have time to walk through the experience with her in a personal way.

Gratefully, Donna's cancer responded to treatment, and after some time she was declared in remission. Then in 2005, the cancer returned. By then my children had all left home, with the youngest still in college, and I was an empty nester, so I had the time and energy to express care for her during her cancer treatments. I went with Donna to her appointments with the oncologist and stayed with her during some of her three-hour chemo sessions. As we sat together in the treatment room, we studied the Bible and prayed.

I am so thankful to have had this time with her. Just by being together our relationship grew in ways that were impossible during her first cancer diagnosis. This experience was a gift from God to both of us in those days, and even more so to me when she eventually succumbed to the disease.

Time is a precious commodity. We cannot grow more of it, but we do have twenty-four hours in every day. How we choose to use our days will vary from season to season. With the advent of the empty nest, we have the opportunity of adjusting our priorities to include more time for siblings.

### Take the Initiative to Strengthen Relationships

We may have been out of touch with our siblings; we may even have unresolved issues with them. We may feel like we don't have much in common or know one another very well. Most likely, we simply haven't had the time or energy to put into these relationships because of our own family's needs. And yet as we age, something in us longs to reconnect.

Take the initiative. Call them. Invite them to visit you. Offer to go see them. Plan a reunion. If your siblings don't respond, reach out to their kids. Your nieces and nephews may long to connect with you, but you may need to make this happen. They are part of the next generation, your legacy. And when you pursue them, you may be paving the way for deeper relationships with your siblings.

Just as forgiveness may be needed in rebuilding ties with our parents, it may also be needed with our siblings. If we have unresolved issues, we may need to ask for forgiveness; if we feel wronged we may need to grant forgiveness. If they're not receptive at first, keep trying. It's the right thing to do.

Years ago something happened to Sue's brother, Bob. He sold his home and moved away with his wife and children. He cut off relationships with his extended family. He would not return calls. Word came to Sue that he no longer wanted anything to do with her or their brother. Although confused and hurt, Sue determined to maintain contact. She sent him birthday and Christmas cards through his children. She asked for forgiveness for any way she might have offended him. She enlisted the prayers of her friends, and she persevered. Five years went by without a word from him. Then out of the blue she got a card. She responded with grace and joy, and then she received a call from his wife, who said how much they wanted to reconnect. To this day Sue does not know what happened, but she knows this miracle is an answer to prayer. Most important, she has chosen to accept him where he is, let the past go, and move forward in building a new relationship.

### Make a Priority of Being Together

BARBARA: Years ago my parents began a tradition of gathering their four children, their spouses, and their kids together every Thanksgiving. It's a lot of work, but even today, my mom, at age ninety-one, continues to host this gathering, believing that it is important to build strong family relationships through all the generations. So each year, thirty to forty of us gather in a hundred-year-old farmhouse with just four bedrooms!

We have rented campers for extra sleeping spaces to accommodate all the adults, and everyone brings sleeping bags and extra pillows for lining up kids on the living room floor. We eat all our meals on paper plates. Touch football, four-wheeling, deer hunting before dawn, and working jigsaw puzzles together give us a chance to laugh and play and get to know one another. We're all ordinary, imperfect individuals with our own struggles, but this time together gives us a sense of being rooted, of belonging, and of being accepted—simply because we *are* family. Not one of us would miss it!

As we transition through the empty nest, many of us will find ourselves thinking more about our last years. The future doesn't seem forever away as it did when we were nursing babies and chasing toddlers. We have experienced more deaths. Our bodies are squeaky. In spite of the best makeup, our wrinkles show, and our bulges are harder to hide. Our future will not be as long as our past. Our days ahead are precious. We want to make them count. We want to be *ready* when God calls us home. Part of being ready involves being reconciled in all of our relationships.

When we lose those we love, we want to look back with a sense of gratitude rather than with feelings of regret. "But you don't know how bad my relationship with this person has been," you might be saying. That's right, we don't. But God does. And He has been there with you even in the most painful times.

Ellen was raised in an abusive home. Her only brother came out as gay, and she also became estranged from her father. Several years later, her brother was diagnosed with AIDS, and in the same week her father was told that he had terminal cancer. Emma felt a desire to encourage and support both her brother and father in their health crises, but she knew that in her father's case, she needed to forgive him before she could help him. It was painful, but with God's tender mercy she forgave her dad, and just before he died he gave his life to Christ and asked for forgiveness. Then as she nursed her brother in his final days, he, too, surrendered his life to a loving heavenly Father who understands pain and who is able to forgive and to restore. Emma's story is one of gratitude for relationships redeemed instead of regret and bitterness for relationships lost.

She has taught us the importance of doing all that we can to care for our extended family—to the very last day.

Will you?

> But if a widow has children or grandchildren, these should learn first of all to put their religion into practice by caring for their own family and so repaying their parents and grandparents, for this is pleasing to God.
>
> 1 Timothy 5:4 NIV

# Take the Next Step

· · · · ·

1. Make a fresh assessment of your parents' needs. See appendix 1 for suggestions.

2. Make plans to reconnect with a sibling or to engage with nieces, nephews, and in-laws.

3. Is there anyone whose forgiveness you need to seek, or someone you need to forgive (even if they haven't sought it)? No matter how long it's been or how bad it's been, it's never too late to do what is right. Begin to live with no regrets.

4. Write a tribute to your parents and in-laws, thanking them for what they did right.

## Recommended Reading

*The Forgotten Commandment: Experiencing the Power of Honoring Your Parents* by Dennis Rainey with Dave Boehi (FamilyLife, 2014)

# Christie's Story

## Surprised by a New Calling . . . and Loving It!

*urprise!*

No word better describes Christie's empty-nest experience.

With their son, Sky, already out of the house, Christie and Steve were looking forward to the freedom to travel and to delve into things they had put off for many years.

A jill-of-all-trades, Christie had worked as an administrative assistant, Bible study leader, children's choir director, and fund raiser. Fulfilling a dream, she also studied with a chef for three years and became a gourmet cook. Always seeking new challenges, Christie approached the empty nest with great expectation.

> Some of my friends were lamenting the fact that their babies were moving on, but I felt joy and freedom—freedom to move to a new phase of life. Even though Sky and I have always been close, he was ready to spread his wings and I was ready for him to experience life. Sky's transition to independence was a celebration for all three of us.

However, dreams and freedom were put on hold when Christie's mother was diagnosed with inoperable lung cancer. Since her parents lived two hours away, Christie began to make frequent visits to help her father take care of her mother. A few days after her mother's first chemotherapy treatment, Christie arrived at her parents' house to find emergency vehicles there. Rushing in the front door, she learned that her dad had collapsed and the paramedics could not revive him.

> Too often we go through life thinking we are in control. In this situation I was reminded that we are not in control, but God is and His plan is perfect. How good it was that I "happened" to arrive right after Daddy died. I was able to be there for my mom in a time that she really needed me. God's

129

grace sustained us through the next several weeks. He sent friends and family to step in and help when we needed it the most.

Christie and Steve immediately moved her mother to live with them so that they could take better care of her. It was not the first time Christie had cared for a suffering family member—long before her mother's illness, Christie was at her mother-in-law's bedside for many days before she succumbed to cancer.

Later, during ShareFest, an event put on by local churches to demonstrate the love of Christ to the community through acts of service, Christie became acquainted with Miss Gladys, a spunky woman of seventy-eight who lived alone. To no one's surprise, a friendship blossomed and Christie began caring for her needs as well.

"When I was young I used to laugh at the 'blue hairs.' I made fun of them because they were such slow drivers. I would never have imagined myself caring for them." But care she does—from helping her mom manage the daily battle with a serious illness to running errands for Miss Gladys.

My tongue still hangs out at times, but our whole family has been blessed by these two women. Our son helped us decorate Miss Gladys's Christmas tree and helped cover her windows with plastic before winter arrived. He's observing that people don't have to fade into retirement. Instead, he's seeing that this season of life can be filled with new opportunities to care and show Christ's love to others. He gets to experience this firsthand with his own interactions with these two women. This is a rich experience for a young adult.

Yes, Christie is surprised at her empty-nest adventure. She didn't expect it to be elder care, but it has become her calling. And she loves it.

I have learned that my job is simply to be a willing vessel. To allow God to use me in whatever way He desires. What He desires will be good for me and for my whole family if I let Him have the freedom to work in me. He has given me a dear friend in Miss Gladys, and Mom and I are closer than ever. Caring for them has brought me great joy.

Through my experience I feel like I'm learning the true meaning of grace and patience. I'm seeing the power of prayer in a fresh way. I see God's provision in small details. He thinks of everything.

# Chapter 8

## What Do I Do With Me?

> Faith is the ceasing from all nature's efforts and all other
> dependence; faith is confessed helplessness casting itself
> upon God's promise and claiming its fulfillment; faith
> is the putting of ourselves quietly into God's hands for
> Him to do His work.
>
> Andrew Murray, *Abiding in Christ*

*W*ho *have I become?*
*What is my purpose now that my kids are gone?*
*Does anyone need me?*
*How do I know what to do next?*
*What am I good at?*
*Where do I start?*

Identity. Didn't we deal with that issue in our teen years? Or in our twenties and thirties when we were adjusting to marriage and the arrival of children? Like Barbara's daughter Ashley, who said when she was very pregnant with her fourth baby, "I don't know what happened to the old Ashley!"

Many of us reached an identity milestone when we turned forty and faced the fact that we were entering "middle age." But most of us did not have the time to worry about it then; we were too busy. We were settled in our role. The job of mother became not just what we did, but who we were. Like leather gloves that get softer and conform to the shape of our hands through years of wear, we grew so accustomed to our role that we became . . . comfortable. We fit the role and the role fit us.

This is why the emptying of our nest is such a shock to our system. When our children leave home, our identity walks out the door with them. Some of us may even feel that "me" dies when "they" leave. And we don't know how to find "me" again.

Facing identity questions at this stage of life is a surprise to most of us. "Midlife crisis" is a term generally associated with men, not women. Yet we women are as unprepared for the quandary we suddenly find ourselves in as a middle-aged man who is forced into early retirement. The physical changes in our bodies, along with the relational changes with our husbands, children, extended families, and friends, leave us feeling confused and wondering who we are—*Is this the end of "me"?*

Some days it feels that way, but we know it's not.

Where is the stability in this season? How do we find our center, our sense of purpose? How do we begin to regroup and rearrange our lives? What are we getting out of bed for each morning?

Let's recognize that, as baffling as they are, these feelings of being lost, of wandering, of not knowing who we are anymore are healthy. Painful, yes, but nonetheless healthy as they signal that there is more to come in life. When we realize we have been getting our identity from our kids or our husbands or our jobs, we can begin to see more clearly the inability of other people or other things to fill the real needs of our souls. And that is a very positive place to be. *We were made for more than motherhood.*

We were all created to know the Creator and to have a relationship with Him. Our real identities are always best seen in relation to God and His purposes for life. He is the One who made us and who knows us best. He is in control.

God has woven the experiences of our lives for His purposes and our good. He is writing a story of redemption in each of us. And He will allow the difficulties, the transitions, and the hollow places in our lives to help us see that we are frail and weak and in need of the Savior, Jesus, His Son.

Even those who are believers in Christ will arrive at the empty nest with regrets because the human heart is "prone to wander," as the old hymn says.[1] Keeping our affections properly aligned with God's will is not always easy.

In order to answer the question of this chapter, *What do I do with me?*, we must first answer *Who am I?* Am I in relationship with the One who created me and knows what is best for me? Am I willing to surrender to the One who is really in control and has been in control all along?

Living the rest of the years God gives us with hope and purpose— and none of us knows how many that will be—begins with a personal relationship with God Himself. British theologian J. I. Packer writes,

> Christianity sees each person as designed for a life beyond this life—
> an endless life which for those who know God will be far richer and
> more joyous than our present life can be, and for which life in this
> world was always meant to be *a preparation*. We were never intended
> to treat this world as home, or live in it as if we would be here forever.[2]

If this world is a preparation for the next, and if God is writing a story in our lives, how do we connect with God and join Him in what He is doing?

Some might say, "I don't understand this spiritual dimension. I don't know if I really know God or if I even want to." Others may think, "I want to know God in a personal way. I know I need His help. How can I be sure that He is in my life?" Some may even wonder, "How can I turn to Him now when I've messed up so badly?"

The empty nest brings us a step closer to the edge of eternity, and if we have not given our lives to Christ, the uncertainty of middle age is an opportune time to take that step. The good news is that it's never too late to start fresh. Regardless of our past, we can be honest with God. He longs for us to run to Him, and He wants us to have complete assurance that He is in our life and that He will lead us and help us.

## Susan's Journey to God

I grew up in a home where God was honored and church attendance was expected. My parents loved each other and loved Christ. They raised their four kids to love the Lord and to serve others.

I took on my parents' faith. I, too, believed in a loving heavenly Father and in His Son, Jesus. However, I thought that if I was a little more good than bad, one day I'd get to be in heaven with Him. I incorrectly assumed that being a Christian was synonymous with being good, so I worked hard at being a little more good than bad. It wasn't until I was in college that a friend asked me a clarifying question.

"Susan," he inquired, "are you a Christian?"

"I think I am, I hope I am, I've always believed," I responded.

"God doesn't want you to *think or hope*," he replied. "He wants you to *know* for sure, with absolute certainty.

"No one can be good enough," he continued. "This is why Christ died on the cross for our sins. It's not about being good. It's about accepting His forgiveness for our sins."

My friend shared with me a verse from the Bible that describes Jesus as if He is standing at the door of my heart and knocking and waiting to be invited in: "Behold, I stand at the door and knock; if anyone hears My voice and opens the door, I will come in to him and will dine with him, and he with Me" (Revelation 3:20).

As we talked, I realized that I had never personally invited Christ into my life. Instead, I'd been depending on an inherited faith—the faith of my parents. It was time to personalize this faith. I still had so many questions, but I knew I had to take this first step. So I simply prayed a prayer asking Christ into my life. For me it wasn't an emotional experience; instead, it was a matter of intentionally moving from an inherited faith to a personal faith. It is an emotional experience for some, but one of the great things about God is that He meets each of us in our own individuality.

Taking this step of faith was merely the beginning. I've had many questions and many doubts. I still do. But I have learned that God isn't thrown by my questions. He's God! He can handle anything I bring to Him.

### Barbara's Journey of Faith

Like many children of the 1950s, I was born into a churchgoing family. Our little midwestern town of ten thousand people had a church of every denomination; the Methodist church was the one the Petersons attended. Because we were there every Sunday, I could sing all the hymns and learned the basics about God. But spiritual things were never discussed in our home. As a result, I viewed everyday life in one realm and God in another, more distant realm. Still, I believed in a God and I believed that somehow He had a plan for my life. I just had no idea how to be connected to Him.

During the fall semester of my sophomore year in college, I met a group of students who seemed different from my friends from high school. They were genuine and warm, and I sensed they had a purpose in life that I lacked. One of the girls invited me to a Bible study, something I'd never done before. I was intrigued, so I went. That night I realized that to be a Christian required a choice on my part. I had no idea there was anything to knowing God other than believing He existed. That I had to make a choice and take action was a foreign concept. Like Susan, I was told by the study leader that I could choose to invite Christ into my life by praying a simple prayer to God. I wanted to go to heaven someday when I died, and I had always desired to know God, so I went back to my dorm room and prayed, asking Jesus into my life.

In the years that followed I realized that, just as I desired in childhood, it was actually possible to be connected to God. I grew in my faith through studying God's Word, the Bible. Today I can't imagine how I would have survived the many trials of my life without God's presence in my life to give me peace and comfort and wisdom. Dennis and I acknowledge that we could have divorced each other in the midst of our struggles if we hadn't known Christ and hadn't believed that He had a plan for our lives. Also, I would have missed a multitude of wonderful experiences, great relationships, and an exciting purpose in life if I had continued living life on my own. I'm so grateful for that decision I made in college to accept Christ and His ways and to follow Him for life. It's made *all* the difference.

At the end of this chapter is a prayer similar to the one that each of us prayed when we asked Christ to come into our lives. We have also reprinted a prayer of faith and surrender from John Wesley. We encourage you to consider taking this step. If it seems right for you at this time, we hope you will ask Christ into your life. If you still have questions, that's okay, too. We've included some helpful hints about growing in a relationship with Christ in appendix 2.

## Second Chances

One of the greatest gifts for our generation is the time we've been given to make things right in our lives. A hundred years ago, most women didn't live much past fifty or sixty years of age. Today many of us will only be near the halfway mark when we turn fifty! Getting to know God and living for Him and His divine purpose for our lives is a unique opportunity for our generation. God loves to give second chances, and perhaps this season of the empty nest is His invitation to you to follow Him and His path from here to eternity.

Making things right with God is the place to start in finding new purpose and passion in life. Making things right with key relationships in your life is the next step many need to take. Diana found this to be the case when she had a heart-to-heart talk with her children:

Only a few years after becoming a Christian, as I was approaching the empty nest, I was at a meeting where I learned more on the subject of forgiveness. I came home knowing that I needed to go to each one of my children and ask them to forgive me. I started out by asking them if they could think of any situation where I had hurt them and had never apologized. I knew that what they remembered might not be the same issues that I remembered and that their responses to this might not be what I had hoped. Each of them shared, and I was able to ask them to forgive me for how I had hurt them. It was a positive time. As a result of my openness, one daughter opened up about a sinful act that she had committed that I knew nothing about. God was with me as I was able to handle my response to this information in a Christlike way.

Our children are now all adults and on their own. Recently, another daughter, with whom I had a strained relationship, referred to that time of my apology and said what a breakthrough it was for her in our relationship. I was amazed that my words were still having an effect on her life into the present.

The empty-nest years can be a great season to grapple with questions about God and to strengthen our relationship with Him and others. It's a season in which we have the opportunity to know Him in a deeper way than ever before and to experience life as He intended. If we want to make the most of this new season and experience His next great adventure, we need to discover Him in fresh ways. He is the one who created us, and He knows the plans He has for us. When we seek Him first, He will reveal Himself and He will guide us to our next purpose.

At the beginning of this chapter were the following questions, and we've answered the last one first—a little unorthodox perhaps, but we'll get to the rest of them in the next four chapters if you'll stay with us!

- Who have I become?
- What is my purpose now that my kids are gone?
- Does anyone need me?

- How do I know what to do next?
- What am I good at?
- Where do I start?

We start with God, the Source, the Author, the Giver, the Beginning of life itself. Knowing Him then leads to learning what He has planned for us to do. It's the path to discovering that new purpose, passion, and the next great adventure!

> But when the goodness and loving kindness of God our Savior appeared, he saved us, not because of works done by us in righteousness, but according to his own mercy, by the washing of regeneration and renewal of the Holy Spirit, whom he poured out on us richly through Jesus Christ our Savior, so that being justified by his grace we might become heirs according to the hope of eternal life.
>
> Titus 3:4–7 ESV

## Take the Next Step

• • • • •

Prayers are not magic formulas, but simply guides to help the seeker on her path to *real* Truth. Read the following prayers and pray the one that most expresses the desire of your heart right now. Or choose option 2 and write your own prayer to God.

1. The first prayer below is a simple prayer to follow if you want to invite Christ into your life. The second is a prayer by John Wesley, founder of the Methodist church, that expresses in another way a person's belief in God and offers words of recommitment

and loyalty to His purposes and ways. May these serve you in a growing relationship with the God who created you.

2. If you write your own prayer to God, be completely honest with Him. Nothing shocks God, because He knows our hearts. For encouragement read these prayers of David: Psalm 34 and Psalm 40. (You might find it helpful to read appendix 2, as well.)

### A Prayer of Believing Faith

*Dear Lord Jesus, I need you. I invite you into my life to be my Lord and Savior. Thank you for dying on the cross for me. Thank you that this painful act of yours has allowed my sins to be forgiven. Thank you for promising that you will never leave me. Thank you that I can know right now that one day I'll be in heaven with you, not because I'm good, but because I'm forgiven.*

### Wesley's Covenant Prayer

I am no longer my own but yours.
Put me to what you will.
Put me to doing. Put me to suffering.
Let me be employed for you,
Or laid aside for you.
Exalted for you,
Or brought low for you.
Let me be full, let me be empty.
Let me have all things,
Let me have nothing.
I freely and wholeheartedly yield
All things to your pleasure and disposal.
And now glorious and blessed God,
Father, Son, and Holy Spirit,
You are mine and I am yours. So be it.
And this covenant now made on earth,
Let it be satisfied in Heaven.
Amen.

John Wesley

## Recommended Reading

*Mere Christianity* by C. S. Lewis (HarperCollins, 1980)

*Lies Women Believe: And the Truth That Sets Them Free* by Nancy Leigh DeMoss (Moody, 2001)

*Basic Christianity* by John Stott (InterVarsity Press, 2012)

*Better Than My Dreams: Finding What You Long for Where You Might Not Think to Look* by Paula Rinehart (Thomas Nelson, 2007)

# Your Story

You've been reading the stories of others and now it's your turn. Why not take a few minutes to write a description of your faith journey? This exercise could help clarify where you have been, where you are, the questions you still have, and how you see God at work. Your story also becomes a treasure for future generations.

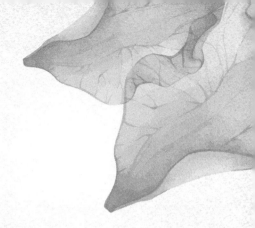

# PART THREE

## Let's Move Forward

# Chapter 9

## Take a Break!

The unexamined life is the wasted life.

Plato

**R**emember the McDonald's commercial from many years ago—"You deserve a break today"? We enthusiastically, wholeheartedly proclaim to you moms who have finished the parenting journey:

**You need a break! Take one!**

This is one of the pillars of our message to you: Women need to take the time to *retreat* and *rest* from the years of mothering, to *recuperate* if necessary, to *reflect* on their lives, and to *refocus* for the future God has planned for them.

Motherhood is much like an ultramarathon race that's run over distances of fifty to one hundred miles or more through harsh terrain like Death Valley or up steep inclines like Mount Whitney. These are long, grueling races that leave the runners near complete exhaustion.

Mothers, like marathoners, sometimes stumble through desert-like seasons and other times enjoy the invigoration of mountaintop vistas. And yes, mothers often reach the finish line exhausted and in desperate need of refreshment.

This is certainly true of most of the women we've interviewed. However, many never realized they needed to rest or that they should (and could) take some time off.

One woman observed that many of us have made surrendering to the wishes of others an art form. We feel guilty if we take any time for ourselves as though *constantly* meeting someone else's needs is the noblest way to live. Many women seem to think like martyrs, always sacrificing for others. While much of that kind of self-sacrifice is required, *God doesn't desire that we live in a constantly depleted state.* He made provision for the refreshment of His people; and we would be wise to follow His pattern by scheduling a season for retreat, rest, and reflection.

## Why Retreat?

*Retreat* means to pull back—as when troops pull back from the front lines of battle in order to regroup and prepare for the next engagement. It does *not* mean surrender; it's just a break in the action. Similarly, we believe that those of you who have served for years on the front line of your family need to retreat and regroup before engaging in your next adventure.

How?

First, you must schedule your retreat. This may be an easy decision, or it may take a good amount of planning to put your job, your family, and other responsibilities on hold for a while. Taking leave necessitates planning and preparation. Remember, you are transitioning from one purpose in life to another, and you don't want to launch into the next season unprepared, ill equipped, or exhausted.

Second, begin to think about what you need in this time of retreat. Do you literally need to leave home and get away? Do you need to cancel some responsibilities or obligations? Do you just need to say no to a long list of requests and stay home? Whatever you choose, we'd recommend that you retreat *intentionally*. Plan for your time of retreat. Gather a stack of books to read—some for fun and some for deeper thinking. Design times and places of quiet comfort. Purpose to begin writing out your thoughts, hopes, fears, and dreams in order to distill the essence of what God is working into your life. And be sure to listen. Listen carefully to the unique longings of your heart and the quiet whisper of God's voice.

Betty wasn't able to take a long time off, but she knew she needed some sort of a personal retreat. As she entered the empty nest, she was bone-tired, a little discouraged, and lacking clarity about her future. A friend had told her about a one-day prayer retreat based on the *Spiritual Exercises of Ignatius of Loyola*. Ignatius was a Jesuit priest in the sixteenth century.

"Simply planning a day just for myself was a luxury for me," Betty says. "It took discipline to put it on the calendar and find a quiet place where I could go. I had to say no to other demands, which wasn't easy, but I knew I needed some time simply to sit with the Lord and to listen to Him for more than fifteen or twenty minutes."

Betty goes on to explain,

> The first exercise during my one-day retreat was to practice thanksgiving by noting ten ways that I experienced God's love at that very moment. I wrote down things like the beauty of the light filtering through the trees, the faithful love of my husband, a rich fellowship of believing friends, good health at age fifty-five. . . . I found that as I took time to note the specifics, I began to realize how personally God loves me.
>
> This was a turning point for me. I've continued to do this from time to time by myself or with a small group of friends, and I have always come away refreshed and encouraged.

### Why Rest?

The pattern God gave for rest can be found in the Old Testament, where He made it clear to His people that He intended for them to work and then rest. Interestingly, God established three different times of rest. One is the weekly ritual most of us are familiar with called the Sabbath.

Many of us grew up in a time when Sunday was a day for going to church, then spending the remainder of the day at home. Because businesses were closed on Sundays, a day of rest was an accepted way of life for most Americans. God set aside one day out of seven in the Old Testament for His people to rest, and that principle was practiced across our nation for generations. God knew humans needed rest regularly, and it was so important that He gave it to us as one of the Ten Commandments.

Let's admit, though, that even when it was common to our culture, most mothers didn't take many Sundays off. Families still had to be fed, homework needed to be done, and more. At least we know that in the Rainey and Yates homes, needs certainly didn't stop on Sundays!

The second kind of rest prescribed in the Old Testament was called the sabbatical year, which occurred every seventh year (mirroring the Sabbath day, which occurred every seventh day). In this sabbatical year, even the land was to rest from being cultivated, which meant that those who worked the land were also more at rest than they were the previous six years (see Leviticus 25:2–7). Life slowed down substantially for these families *if* they practiced this pattern.

The third prescribed time for rest and restoration was the year of Jubilee. This was to be a season of freedom for all, celebrated after the seventh seven-year period, or at the end of forty-nine years. The fiftieth year was a grand occasion, a time for the people to rest and to remember who owned their lives and their destiny. It was a year to celebrate the freedom that comes when one's life belongs to God.

It's wonderful to know that God in heaven understands what we need and that He has planned for us to have seasons of rest. Our problem is that we, like the children of Israel, don't follow God's plan very well. Most of us don't even rest for a full day each week. Can you imagine taking off an entire year?

But rest is precisely what women need as we begin this new season of life. It's time to press the pause button, to step outside our hectic lives for a time to retreat, rest, and reflect in order to let God lead us beside still waters, to restore our souls (see Psalm 23:2–3). This can take place in a short time frame (like Betty's one-day retreat), a weekend away, or a month. For others, this time of rest and reflection may take up to a year. The pattern will vary according to the individual, but for every woman, it is needed.

### Phyllis's Year of Jubilee

The year Phyllis turned fifty, even though she was not quite at the empty nest, she took a year's leave of absence from teaching high-school special education to celebrate her year of Jubilee. Phyllis said of her decision,

I would walk through the halls of the school thinking, "This is a great job with benefits, and it has allowed me to be with my kids, but there is more to my life than this. This job has consumed me for over twenty years, but it's not the real me." It was difficult to make the decision to take a year off, to set aside the security, the stability, the recognition, and the routine, but it has been such a good decision. I'm taking classes at a junior college and being stretched out of my comfort zone, and that's been good.

### A Whole Year Off?

Lois said,

I had heard the advice, encouraging moms to take up to a year off after their last child left home, but I couldn't imagine doing that. The idea of taking a year off seemed far too extreme for my personality. After eight-plus years of homeschooling, I feared I would feel lost and purposeless without activities on my schedule. However, when that fall arrived, I had absolutely nothing on my plate! It worked out beautifully. I was so surprised to find that I actually enjoyed being home alone and doing some of the things I had put off for years. I expected to feel restless if I didn't quickly have a sense of direction. Instead, God has given me a great sense of peace and contentment to wait for His leading.

Betty, Phyllis, and Lois illustrate both ends of the spectrum of rest and retreat. It can be done in one day or one year. Most of us will need and want to design something in between, like Leslie, who wasn't able to take a year's leave of absence from her career but did plan for a weekend away with three other women. Or like Tina, who met with a group of a dozen women in a retreat setting to seek to know the next step in their lives. This group of women participated in the classical practice of *Lectio Divina* (Latin for "divine reading"), a tradition of listening to God's Word as it is read aloud.

Tina has found, and we agree, that we need to create space in our lives in which we can listen to Jesus and let Him breathe fresh life into our weary souls. He cherishes our company and loves for us to make space for Him. He wants to be with us. Our tendency is to neglect the value of being *with Him* because we are often too busy doing *for Him*. Tina's passion is to help women enjoy being with Jesus and to grow in valuing solitude and silence as a meeting place with Him.

One of our favorite (and most convicting!) Scriptures is "Be still, and know that I am God" (Psalm 46:10 ESV). A regular part of a time of rest and retreat should involve listening. Both of us long to practice this more regularly.

### Barbara's Season of Rest

As I entered the empty-nest season, I knew because of the exhausting journey with our prodigal daughter that I was depleted emotionally and physically. I needed a break, but I had no idea how to take one. At the same time, Dennis was thrilled with the idea of having me back to himself after all the years of sharing me with the kids. I was genuinely looking forward to having more time with him, as I'd heard friends talk about the fun they were having with their husbands. But I also knew I wanted more for the second half of my life than just following my husband around. I felt a bit guilty for wanting more—after all, I love and respect my husband—but I couldn't ignore the feelings. At the time, I couldn't sort them all out anyway. I was too tired.

Since the day I became a mother, like many of you, I'd spent most of my waking hours meeting the needs of others. I had deliberately chosen to delay the fulfillment of my personal gifts and talents in order to be fully available to my children and husband. Now, it was time to regroup.

I told Dennis that I wanted some time off; but he was thinking a few weeks, and I was thinking much longer. In hindsight neither of us, but especially my husband, had any idea how depleted I was from the trials of our daughter's rebellion and from the sheer volume of needs I'd been meeting for our six kids over the past twenty-eight-plus years.

After talking about this together, we agreed I should take a break from the hectic pace of our lives. For six months I shifted my focus from the activity of meetings, travel, and tasks to the "work" of restoring my soul. My goal was to slow my pace and allow my mind, body, and soul to recuperate from the years of motherhood. Because we travel a lot in our work, I didn't need to go somewhere; instead, I needed to stay home. I took an art class for the first time in twenty-five years and an in-depth Bible study class—delighted to be home so that I could attend every session. I allowed myself the luxury of sleeping in if I needed to, and I established a regular exercise routine. I also began some self-assessment of my strengths and weaknesses, gifts and talents for the purpose of knowing how to best maximize my life in the next season. (We'll give some tips on how to do this in chapter 11.) Those classes and the break from the pressures of work were therapy for my soul. Expressing my latent gifts gave me joy I'd not had in years.

My season of rest was not as concentrated as a weekend or a week away with an intense focus on meeting with God. Mine was more gradual, as I still had all my normal household tasks and duties and continued involvement in my adult children's lives. But it was what I needed, and that—knowing what we each need as an individual—is the key.

As mothers, our tendency is to see the empty spaces in our schedule when the last child leaves and think we need to fill those spaces immediately with other activities or tasks. That's what our friend Elise did.

Elise thought she was being wise about the upcoming empty nest and scheduled her fall calendar with new committees to serve on, a volunteer outreach to be a part of, and several other activities. She didn't realize that when her last child left home, much of her motivation would walk out the door as well. After two months of this new level of activity, Elise found herself crashing into depression; her tears didn't stop. Elise had made some incorrect assumptions about herself. She did not foresee any need for rest, and she did not understand that grief would be part of her transition.

To ease your transition, take the time to rest, listen to the longings of your heart, and listen for the voice of God. It is the key to discovering the next great adventure God has for *you*. With enough planning, it is possible to arrange a season of retreat and rest so that you can prepare for the future. Do whatever you can afford, both financially and professionally, to schedule a break for yourself. God will guide in what you need to do.

Now is the time to stop and pick up some of those set-aside interests. Now is the time to refuel. One of our greatest encouragements and joys is to say to you, Do this for yourself. Don't stay on the treadmill of activity. Stop. Get off. Take a break!

## Why Reflect?

The purpose of a time of reflection is to evaluate your life thus far, to assess the challenges you currently face, and to begin to discover that new passion you long for at this stage of life. Give yourself the time to honor the transition. Think about the changes that are coming and how you feel about them.

We challenge you, in this time of retreat, to reflect on the past, the present, and the future.

### Reflect on the Past With Gratitude

Central to God's purpose for His people's sabbatical rest was the opportunity to remember all that He had done in their personal and collective history. When we truly focus on His goodness, our response is ultimately one of gratitude and worship. Reflection reminds us that God has been and still is in control, that He oversees everything in our lives even when it may feel to us that things are spinning out of control. Reflecting on God puts all of life in perspective.

A good way to approach your time of reflection is by journaling or by just making a list of the ways God has worked in your life in the past. Keep adding to your list or journal as your memory is refreshed. Record all you can think of that God has done. Like David said in the psalms, "Give thanks to the Lord, for He is good" (see Psalm 106:1; 107:1; 118:1; 136:1).

Giving thanks is helpful no matter what season of life you are in; but especially at this transitional mark, ask God to help you focus on all that is good in your life, to remember all the ways you have overcome difficulties and all the ways you have seen Him at work. This is something God's children have done for generations to help them remember His faithfulness. The psalms of the Bible are records in song of God's mighty deeds; they were written to remind God's people of the truth about His nature—and the truth about their own.

Perhaps you can write a psalm of gratitude to God for all He has done.

### Reflect on Your Life Story

Another way to approach reflection is to write those personal recollections that bubble to the surface from the story of your life. This, too, can be helpful in discovering your new purpose and passions.

In his book *To Be Told: Know Your Story, Shape Your Future*, Dan Allender writes,

> There never has been nor ever will be another life like mine—or like yours. Just as there is only one face and name like mine or yours, so there is only one story like mine. And God writes the story of my life to make something known about himself, the One who wrote me. The same is true of you. Your life and mine not only reveal who we are, but they also help reveal who God is.[1]

The first goal of this season of rest and reflection is to help you discover the significance of what God is writing and working in your life so you can know what direction He has planned for your future. As Sam says to Frodo (in *The Two Towers*), "I wonder what sort of a tale we've fallen into?"[2]

What is the theme of your tale, your life story?

From the beginning of your life, God placed you into a story where He would shape you largely by things that were beyond your control—painful circumstances, hard choices, and unpredictable people—using the good and the bad of all types of things to sculpt your life for His grand design. Understanding the impact of significant life experiences and the influence of key people is important in determining your future direction. They have molded who you have become. Also, identifying the recurring themes in your life will help uncover the passions God wants you to pursue in the future.

But just as the children of Israel—whose history is recorded in the Old Testament—failed many times to obey God, we, too, may be forced through our reflection to remember that at times we turned away from God's ways and went off on our own, creating pain and suffering for ourselves and others. Sometimes the solitude of an empty house brings to the surface issues that we buried while we raised our kids—past mistakes we never dealt with in the tyranny of life, relationships we let slide because we did not want a confrontation, personal struggles we overlooked because we were preoccupied with kid issues. Now some of these matters may resurface, and that can hurt. Be prepared.

156

### *Reflect on the Past With Courage*

A dear friend of ours, Pat, has a remarkable story to tell.

During the four-year time span between when our first went to college
and the last one left home, I lost my mom, completed menopause,
stopped hormones cold turkey, experienced 9/11, changed churches
after twenty years, and was forced to close the fifty-year-old family
business due to my bankrupt bipolar brother's neglect. That action
led me to join a friend in a new business that ultimately failed. During all this I made the decision to leave my husband, who had been
abusive for years. Instead, he got help and I changed my mind about
leaving. It was also during this time that God had me encounter His
healing for two abortions in my past. Helping post-abortive women
like me has now become my passion. In the words of Beth Moore, I
finally handled my stuff!

In the years since *Roe v. Wade* became law in 1972, we've gone
from naïvely thinking abortion was a simple solution without consequences to having a growing understanding that the emotional
aftershocks of abortion can last a lifetime for both men and women.
Post-abortion syndrome s a type of post-traumatic stress disorder.
As a culture, we are just waking up to the personal anguish and
potential fallout these disorders represent.

We mention this because a life-altering experience of this mag-
nitude affects everything: your marriage, your children, your job,
and your relationship with God. Because the empty nest can be a
significant time to reflect, it may be the best opportunity you've
had to finally pursue healing if abortion—or some other trauma—is
in your past. The empty nest affords you more time to think than
you've had in years, and you may be surprised by the issues that
begin to surface that you've managed to keep buried during the
busy years of parenting.

As Pat went on to say, "There is a significant difference between
forgiveness and genuine healing," and so we encourage you to take
the risk and pursue healing for your soul. (See the list of resources
for healing from post-abortion syndrome at the end of this chapter.)

There is a wonderful eternal truth that applies to this and any other heartache. It's a promise that says, "God causes all things to work together for good to those who love God, to those who are called according to His purpose" (Romans 8:28). He has a plan for each of our lives, and He can and will use all of our story and life experiences for great good.

Pat is now actively involved in helping other women find healing and hope from past abortions. She is passionate about this new calling in her life, this opportunity to see good come from a dark place in her life story. As you consider your own regrets and dark places, please remember that nothing is too hard for God (see Luke 1:37). He can redeem anything, anyone, anytime. Will you let Him?

### Reflect on the Present in Light of God's Faithfulness

We've talked in previous chapters about the conflicting emotions and challenging situations common to the empty-nest experience. In reflecting on your life in the present, focus on where you are struggling or feeling the greatest need for growth and stability.

SUSAN: As I hit the empty nest, a time I found most difficult was early morning. Since I was no longer awakened by toddlers needing immediate attention or having to push teens out the door to get to school on time, it was easy to wake up and focus on myself and my to-do list. Too often I found myself feeling blue even before I got out of bed.

I realized that I needed to do something to get myself out of this pit. And I knew that the place to start was focusing on *who God is* rather than on myself. So I began to ask God to give me one character trait of His to focus on each day. One particular morning the trait was *God is our Rescuer.* As I went to the kitchen to fix a cup of tea, my phone rang. On the line was a friend in tears about her teenage son. "I just feel he needs to be rescued," she exclaimed. What a sweet conversation we had about our heavenly Father, the Rescuer.

From time to time I say God's character traits out loud. Simply remembering who He is and thanking Him is a way of building faith and of focusing my thoughts where they need to be. It's like filling up a bucket with refreshing water rather than loading it with stones of worry and self-reliance.

Another time I was on an airplane traveling home from a conference, and I was exhausted. In my depleted state, I began to worry about one of my college-age children. The more I thought about this child, the more my imagination wandered. I tried to pray, but that only caused me to worry more. Finally I cried out to God in desperation, "Help me!" I did not hear His voice audibly, but what came into my mind was startlingly clear—a simple phrase, "Remember Me." At that point I realized that my specific concern about my child had grown bigger in my mind than my God. I had forgotten who He is—the Father who knows my child better than I do, the God for whom nothing is impossible, the God from whom nothing is hidden, the God with unlimited power.

When I focused on who He is, my concern about my child began to diminish. Of course, the problem was still there, but it wasn't blown out of proportion. Seeing my concern in light of God's love and faithfulness gave me a fresh perspective, and my heart was calmed again.

In appendix 3 we have included a guide that has a different trait of God for you to focus on each day for a month. We hope this will help you begin to reflect on His faithfulness.

### Reflect on the Future and Its Possibilities

As you begin to imagine the future, make lists of your ideas, dreams, hopes, fears, questions, and plans. Record all the things you'd like to do with the rest of your life, places you'd like to visit, books you want to read, skills you want to learn. Nothing is off limits. You may never get to it all, but this is part of the journey of discovery. It's time to begin to dream again. And be sure to dream with your husband. Dream together and dream often. This is the really fun part of this season.

As Patricia's last child left home, she and her husband planned for an extended trip with two objectives. One was to celebrate this new season, their relationship, and to enjoy some time alone together. The second objective was to investigate new avenues of mission.

Recently Patricia sent an email about their experience that they believe is a foretelling of work they want to do as a couple.

> We've had an incredible two months and have once again been caught up in what God is doing in other parts of the world. Our time in certain countries has allowed us to see the international needs of trafficked women and children. It has been a tremendous honor to sit with people who have given their lives to helping prostitutes and victims of trafficking taste the kindness of Jesus in the midst of their daily darkness.

What adventures of mercy might God have planned for you and your husband in your new season of life? What mission of love and grace might you be a part of for the rest of your life?

We'll discuss this much more in chapter 11, but for now in your time of retreat, rest, and reflection, begin to think and dream about your future.

There is a story about missionaries in Africa who were traveling across the continent. They had hired some men from a certain tribe to serve as their porters, carrying their luggage and other belongings. The first day of the trip, the missionaries were surprised at the record time they made. The porters had moved much faster than they had planned, so their expectations were raised of finishing the journey in half the time. The next morning the missionaries were up early and ready to move on. The porters, however, were not moving and had no interest in pushing ahead. Finally, after much work at communicating, the porters made it clear that while they had made record time the previous day, they would not be starting out again until their *souls caught up with their bodies*.[3]

What a lesson. These tribesmen were willing to take the time to rest. They felt it was necessary—that it was wise to arrive at their destination sound in body and soul.

We women need time—time to step outside our lives to think and reflect on what God has written on our hearts and to listen for His leading for the rest of our lives.

The empty nest often marks the halfway point in our lives. The Psalms tell us, "The years of our life are seventy, or even by reason of strength eighty" (Psalm 90:10 ESV). Let's take the time to be refreshed and get ready for the second half—and the next great adventure.

> Remember the sabbath day, to keep it holy. Six days you shall labor and do all your work, but the seventh day is a sabbath of the Lord your God; in it you shall not do any work. . . .
>
> Exodus 20:8–10

# Take the Next Step

Just as you are unique as an individual created in God's image, so you will walk a unique and personal path in this empty-nest season. We trust you will personalize the list below to fit your needs and resources. This is not a formula, but rather principles that, when practiced, will help each woman discover God's purposes for the rest of her life.

1. Plan a time of retreat. Following the suggestions in this chapter, take some time to get away by yourself to think, pray, and seek God's direction for your life. Be intentional!

2. Collect a few books, both for fun and for guidance. Refer to our recommended resource lists for ideas.

3. Plan for some time of reflection while on your personal retreat. Use the following questions to help you think through your

life from the past to the present, and then begin to imagine the future. These are not simple questions, and you should not try to answer them quickly. Take your time. Don't feel you have to answer them all. This is to warm your brain—not fry it.

### Questions for Reflection

Where have I found my identity in the past?

Who have I become as I have raised my children?

What have been the longings of my heart since childhood?

When have I felt most alive and significant in the past?

Are there any secrets that need to be uncovered and finally dealt with?

Why do I really do the things that I do?

What motivates me?

What must I eliminate in my life?

What must stay the same?

What do I need to add?

What dreams have I had that I've not had the time to pursue?

What makes my life meaningful?

What in life do I most desire?

Write a psalm of gratitude for all that is positive in your life, from as far back as you can recall to the present. If you have never written a psalm, consider using the opening words of Psalm 106 as a place to start: "Praise the Lord! Oh give thanks to the Lord, for He is good." List ways that God has shown His goodness to you or begin writing about a time when you experienced His goodness.

### Recommended Reading

*To Be Told: Know Your Story, Shape Your Future* by Dan Allender (Waterbrook, 2005)

*Her Choice to Heal: Finding Spiritual and Emotional Peace After Abortion* by Sydna Massé (David C. Cook, 2008)

*A Praying Life* by Paul Miller (NavPress, 2009)

### Barbara and Susan's Favorite Reads for a Retreat

*1000 Gifts* by Ann Voscamp (Zondervan, 2011)

*Jesus Calling: Enjoying Peace in His Presence* by Sarah Young (Thomas Nelson, 2004)

*Choosing Rest* by Sally Breedlove (NavPress, 2002)

*Abide in Christ* by Andrew Murray (Whitaker House, 1979)

*Windows of the Soul* by Ken Gire (Zondervan, 1996)

*Prayer: Finding the Heart's True Home* by Richard Foster (Harper Collins, 1992)

*Gift From the Sea* by Anne Morrow Lindbergh (Random House, 1975)

Any books by C. S. Lewis

*Don't Waste Your Life* by John Piper (Crossway Books, 2003)

*The Valley of Vision: A Collection of Puritan Prayers and Devotions* by Arthur G. Bennett (The Banner of Truth Trust, 1975)

*Radical Gratitude: Discovering Joy Through Everyday Thankfulness* by Ellen Vaughn (Zondervan, 2005)

### Barbara and Susan's Fun Reads

Books by Peter Mayle, especially *A Year in Provence* (1991 reprint edition), *Toujours Provence* (1992 reprint edition), *Chasing Cézanne* (1998 reprint edition) (Vintage Books)

*The Emerald Mile: The Epic Story of the Fastest Ride in History Through the Heart of the Grand Canyon* by Kevin Fedarko (Scribner, 2013)

*The Boys in the Boat: Nine Americans and Their Epic Quest for Gold at the 1936 Berlin Olympics* by Daniel James Brown (Viking, 2013)

*Unbroken: A World War II Story of Survival, Resilience, and Redemption* by Laura Hillenbrand (Random House, 2010)

Novels by Randy Alcorn, including *Deadline* (2006 reprint edition), *Dominion* (2006 reprint edition), *Deception* (2007 reprint edition) (Multnomah), *Safely Home* (Tyndale, 2011 paperback edition)

Novels by Ted Dekker, including *Black, Red,* and *White* (Thomas Nelson, 2009 anniversary editions)

Novels by Joel Rosenberg (Tyndale, various)

Bug Man series (various) and *Plague Maker* (2006) by Tim Downs (Thomas Nelson)

# Debbie's Story

## Never Too Old to Love Kids

Debbie turned fifty the year her youngest son graduated from high school. That same year, her family moved from the East Coast to the West Coast. With so many changes, she didn't have time to contemplate becoming an empty nester. Then her sister encouraged her to take a sabbatical year. So Debbie, recalling the history of the children of Israel from Leviticus 25, celebrated "a year of Jubilee."

She decided not to commit to anything for a year. Instead, she spent time with Jesus, took time getting to know her new community, reconnected with extended family, and focused on her marriage.

At the end of the year, she took a part-time job at a small European-style boutique where olive oil from local Sonoma olives was made and sold.

> The women I worked with in the shop were so unlike me. They weren't followers of Jesus. Several were into new age spiritualism; I appreciated these women—their questions and searching. I loved getting to know the area through their eyes. It was a broadening experience for me. I learned much from these colleagues. And even though just one of us still works there, we continue to care for each other and have stayed connected.

Debbie began to think about what she might do next. When her boys had been in high school, she had worked as a guidance counselor. She had discovered that she loved working with teens, loved listening to them, and loved helping them. She wondered if there were any opportunities for her to work with teens again. She had come to know a number of adults who were concerned about the tremendous needs of the youth in the area. Several had a desire to begin a local Young Life[4] ministry for the middle-school kids. Her brother-in-law was willing to help them begin, and Debbie decided that she could be a prayer partner.

"I didn't feel I was suited to be a leader. I'm not an extrovert. I don't like speaking in front of people. I'm not funny. And all of these things are important for a Young Life leader. But I could pray."

Debbie began to pray, and a group of untrained, mostly over-fifty adults began to reach out to hurting sixth through eighth graders. A few months later Debbie reluctantly joined the other leaders in taking thirteen of the kids to camp.

> It was a real stretch for me. We had a fourteen-hour bus ride to camp; and when we finally arrived, I quickly learned firsthand one of Young Life's core values—earning the right to be heard. At midnight I got thrown in the swimming pool with my clothes on! But it was a week that changed my life because I saw God reach down and change the lives of kids.

It wasn't long before Debbie found herself—at age fifty-two—the area director of Young Life.

> One of the scariest things about my job was having to raise financial support. But I felt God was saying to me, "Don't think about how you *feel* about it, just do it. I will provide." And He did.
>
> During the past five years I have had the privilege of seeing God change lives. I first met Trina when she was thirteen. I went to watch her play volleyball. Because she did not have a stable family, she lived with whoever was willing to take her in for short periods of time. By all standards she should not have made it. But she came to Young Life and she came to our camps. We loved her and cared for her, and she finally earned her high school diploma. Today she's nineteen and working as a teaching assistant while volunteering with at-risk youth. (At the moment she's visiting me for a couple of days with a friend. When I awoke this morning, I found them both already up at my kitchen table studying their Bibles together.) I marvel at what God has done.

Debbie says she's learned that God simply wants our hearts to be tender toward what He wants. "It doesn't matter that we are ill equipped, old, or raw. We are never too old to love kids. And kids are not put off by our age; instead, they are drawn by our love."

# *Chapter 10*

# Celebrate!

The most evident token and apparent sign of true wisdom *is a constant and unconstrained rejoicing.*

Michel de Montaigne (emphasis added)

SUSAN: When our twin daughters married within six weeks of each other, it was the third summer in a row of Yates weddings. These two were the last ones. Soon the nest was going to be really empty. Thinking about the summer ahead, I suspected that there would be a big letdown after Libby's wedding, the final one.

I knew we would all be exhausted after two big weddings, but I also knew I'd be sad. I suspected it would be easy for John and me to simply dive into cleanup mode and settle back into the responsibilities of life. At the same time, I imagined that we would need an emotional lift, a time of intentionally celebrating *us* as we began our empty nest.

So we decided that two days after the wedding we would go on our own honeymoon! Friends loaned us their beach house. We left thank-you notes undone and our cluttered house still a mess to go celebrate our new freedom. Yes, I felt some sadness and fear, but also a sense of anticipation. John surprised me by renting a bright red convertible, and we drove off into the sunset with the top down—pretending we were the bride and groom!

During our time away we went into a little chapel by ourselves, knelt by the altar, and went through the marriage service again as a way of rededicating ourselves to one another afresh in this new season. We read Psalm 112, which particularly spoke to this time in our lives. This simple act began to lessen my anxiety about marriage in the empty nest and sowed seeds of excitement that good things were ahead.

In our busy lives, it's easy to forget to celebrate. After all, there are so many demands and so little time. Yet the children of Israel often took time to celebrate—and this was by God's design!

### God's People Throw a Party!

The people had worked hard and fast, and now it was time to celebrate. Nehemiah and Ezra sent out invitations for a grand party for thousands of people. Some of their friends were singers, so they came to give a concert. Others brought food and gifts. Some families cleaned while others decorated. Some chipped in to help with finances. There was singing and dancing and a real live parade right on the top of the newly finished walls of Jerusalem. The Scriptures were read aloud to the guests. Children of all ages joined in to celebrate, and the noise was great![1]

Why all the fuss?

For generations the children of Israel had been forced to live in exile in Babylon. When the king of Babylon finally allowed them to return, the people were glad to be home, but too dispirited to rebuild the city. It wasn't until Nehemiah returned with prayer, a pep talk, and organizational skills that the work of rebuilding the wall began. After just fifty-two days, the wall around the city was completed—something the people never thought they could accomplish. A celebration was certainly in order. God had been faithful.

168

And oh, what a party they had on top of their new wall!

Partying wasn't that unusual for the children of Israel. In fact, just as they had been commanded by God to observe the Sabbath rest, they had also been instructed to celebrate. God had even given to Moses, their leader, specific details on particular celebrations. And not just for one celebration, but for many throughout the year and some over a period of years.[2] There were festivals to celebrate seasons, harvests, completed projects, protection, and many other occasions.

Celebrations continued after the birth of Christ. Jesus Himself attended a wedding party at Cana, and He used celebrations as examples in His teaching: An overjoyed dad celebrated the return of his wayward son with a huge bash. A woman who lost a coin and found it while cleaning her house threw a party with all her friends—even the angels in heaven celebrate.

Most cultures have a history of celebrations. Indeed, there seems to be something in our human nature that cries out to celebrate, yet we often overlook these opportunities. We're pretty good at observing the big holidays, birthdays, and anniversaries, but other milestones are neglected. We're so driven to move on to the next thing that we give little thought to or thanksgiving for what has been done.

We celebrate our kids' birthdays with parties, we celebrate their graduations with more parties, we celebrate a friend's new baby with a shower, we celebrate weddings with parties galore, but do you know of anyone who has hosted a party to celebrate her arrival at the empty nest? Do we congratulate one another at this season of life? Or do we just ignore this transition as if it were meaningless?

Maybe, just maybe, we need to take a page from the ancient cultures and celebrate!

## Celebrate With Your Husband

Even though we women often feel the brunt of the empty nest more than our husbands do, this season represents a "finishing" for them as well.

BARBARA: Two weeks after Dennis and I dropped off our daughter at college and four weeks after leaving another daughter at rehab, we were off for a planned getaway to celebrate the beginning of the empty nest.

We were exhausted and emotionally spent, but as we drove away, we were suddenly overwhelmed with a silly sense of relief that we actually got to take this trip. We looked at each other in gleeful anticipation and spontaneously gave each other a big high-five!

The onset of this new season allows us a little more time to focus on ourselves, but it also allows us more time to focus on our husbands. Once again, we have a choice whether to concentrate on the negatives or to celebrate the positives. Giving thanks in all things, as we discussed previously, also relates to our spouses.

Years ago, I realized that when I focused on all the things I wished and wanted changed in my husband, all I thought about were those negatives. So I learned to set aside those nuisances and instead notice the things that were good in his life and in our circumstances. It made for a much more positive relationship. And the same is true for our empty-nest years. We all know older people, both men and women, who are unendingly critical, negative, and grumpy. Who wants to be around them? Who wants to be like them? But if we aren't careful to focus on and celebrate the positives in this season, we will follow in their footsteps. As wives, we would do well to remember that thankfulness is like a marriage vitamin—a regular dose strengthens the union.

While getting away together is a great way to celebrate with your husband, perhaps the biggest need for many couples is relearning how to have fun together, as we talked about in chapter 5.

In the seriousness of life, you may feel that you've forgotten how to have fun. Both of us have felt this way. We used to do silly things with our husbands and laugh. But somehow life got so complex that laughter was often set aside. Oh, how we need to capture the freedom of doing silly things and laughing at ourselves again.

If we recapture a sense of playfulness or adventure with our spouses, we will find ourselves enjoying our marriage-friendship again. Establishing simple new routines, new traditions, or new ideas can be helpful.

We asked some friends to offer ideas to get us started. Here are some of their thoughts:

- Choose a new hobby together—something neither of you has done. Try it at least twice.
- Go on walks together.
- Eat by candlelight.
- Use your good china and have friends or newlyweds over for dinner. (You may need to start collecting some, especially if pieces of yours have been broken over the years!)
- Take turns planning a special date night. Keep the plans a surprise.
- Visit your local bookstore/coffee shop. Go to the travel section and design your dream vacation. (Even if you never take it, it's fun to dream together!)
- Make a playlist of your favorite songs. Take a drive in the country and listen to those favorite tunes as you relax on the road.
- Eat dinner in a different room in your home.
- Attend a lecture together at a local college or a demonstration at a home improvement store.
- Learn something new together, like Italian cooking.
- Take turns reading a book out loud.
- Play card games or board games together.
- Start a book club together with some other couples.

It's fun to compile your own list of ideas. It's even more fun to come up with a list with your husband or some creative friends. Choose one thing to try this week or this month. Next month try another.

The key: Be intentional. If we aren't intentional in taking time to celebrate and have fun, we will simply fall into old patterns. If you are already into the empty nest and feeling a bit stale in your marriage, start now! It's never too late.

## Celebrate With Girlfriends

A godly, vivacious grandmother wrote this advice to a friend of ours as she approached the empty nest:

> Yes, the empty nest is very hard and painful, and it lasts all of two weeks! Then, you'll run outside, throw your hat into the air, and say, "I DID IT!" You'll be busier than ever, and having more fun than you can remember. But during those two weeks of grieving, your husband will be no help at all. That's why we have girlfriends.

Your sadness may last a bit longer than two weeks, but the truth is, it's your girlfriends who will best understand your feelings and help you through the rough times. They'll also be more likely to understand the need for a celebration.

BARBARA: If someone had told me to have a party right after Laura left, I would have said, "You're crazy." That's the last thing I felt like doing. I was conflicted. Yes, I was excited about the prospect of the future, but I was feeling sad that my last child was gone. My tendency was to think, *I can't celebrate until I'm happy and only happy.*

But then I thought about weddings—they usually bring mixed emotions. There are tears of joy and tears of sadness as one of life's biggest transitions takes place. That's acceptable. We need to have the same freedom in the empty nest to feel both joy and sadness, to laugh and cry, often within the space of a few minutes. Celebrating is not about waiting until you are happy. It's about celebrating another of life's transitions that is a messy mix of emotions. Celebrating with girlfriends gives us an opportunity to connect emotionally with others who can identify with our feelings.

In doing research for this book, both of us had several get-togethers to which we invited several women who were approaching or already in the empty nest. While we learned so much from them, several were quick to say, "Thanks for having me over! It was so good to hear other women speak honestly about their feelings without being judged. I realized I'm normal, and that is a great relief."

It's time for us to give the empty nest a new reputation—a unique celebration. We're celebrating fresh starts—in our marriages, with our kids, and in anticipation of our own new calling. And we, like the children of Israel, are celebrating God's faithfulness of the past.

Since it is other women who best understand this transition, let's kick off this season with some girlfriends! We asked several of our most creative friends to help us dream up two fantastic empty-nest parties and a getaway.

### *Event #1: An Empty-Nest Celebration!*

**Purpose:** To throw a party that will mark this event as a positive transition into your next great adventure.

**Theme:** New Directions Party—Come Celebrate the Empty Nest!

**Guests:** Invite other moms you have connected with through ball games, church, carpool, the PTA, the marketplace, or homeschool functions.

**Invitations:**
- **Front:** Use a road map with a large question mark drawn across it.
- **Inside text:** "Wondering where to go from here?" (or "Heading in a new direction?") "Let's consider the possibilities together. Can't wait to see you for coffee" (or lunch or tea). Include date, time, and location, and with the RSVP, note: "Come with an idea for a ministry to pursue, a great volunteer opportunity, a timely course to take, etc."

**Suggestion:** Lighten your workload by including several hostesses.

**Dress:** Casual. Or suggest a theme: "Come in the worst outfit you ever wore in a carpool (pajamas, ball cap, etc.)" or "Come dressed for your next 'dream' profession."

**Decor:** Mimic a road by covering the table with black vinyl or oil cloth covers. Stripe it down the center with yellow duct or masking tape. Place toy cars and trucks on the table. Have name tags—they ease introductions and cover memory loss. Write big!

**Program Options:**

- **Possibilities:** Have each person share something she likes about the empty nest and the new "possibility" she brought.
- **People Bingo:** Create bingo cards using info that the hostess knows about her guests as the answers (soccer mom, entrepreneur, PTA president, etc.). Include generic questions as well. (If this idea feels cheesy to you, search the Internet for icebreaker ideas that fit your party. )

### Event #2: An Empty-Nest Discussion

**Purpose:** A simple, low-key way to engage others in a lively discussion about what we are experiencing as we approach the empty nest. To encourage one another to dream about making this new season count significantly for kingdom purposes.

**Theme:** A free-for-all discussion for women in various phases of the empty nest

**Guests:** Invite women in different stages of the empty nest. This might include some women you don't know very well. Use the commonality of your season to reach out to women you don't ordinarily spend time with. You might want to invite a couple of women who are well into their empty-nest years and ask them to share lessons they have learned.

**Invitations:** A simple electronic invitation is sufficient, or send a card that says, "Come join us for a lively discussion on the challenges and benefits of the empty-nest season. Let's dream about our next great adventures." Include time, date, and location, and provide RSVP options.

You could hold this event in your local coffee shop.

**Suggestion:** Ask a friend to host it with you.

**Dress:** Casual

**Decor and Food:** Keep it simple. Serve beverages and finger desserts. Include name tags.

**Program:** Begin by having each guest introduce herself and tell briefly where she is in the season. Then open the time up for discussion, asking two specific questions: (1) "What have been some of your challenges as you've approached or entered the empty nest?" and (2) "What have been some of the benefits?"

Additional option: Discuss ways you can make a significant impact in the world in this new season.

Follow-up: You might reconvene in a few weeks, with each person assigned to share about a project or ministry in which she is hoping to make a difference. Discuss how you can support one another.

Our friend Christi has hosted an empty-nest discussion group for eight years. Every fall, she invites women whose last child just graduated from high school. Invitations go out to everyone she knows from church, the neighborhood, and schools, and she encourages them to invite others. Her guests often don't know one another. Some are believers and some are not. They meet weekly for six or seven weeks, and they always begin with dinner. She says, "The dinner has been very popular because it gives us time to simply visit, getting to know each other. We have name tags, and I have some icebreakers to facilitate conversation." Christi cooks for the first session, and after that other moms sign up to bring food.

They begin each meeting by listening to a radio interview with us about this book.[3] Each twenty-minute segment, recorded for *FamilyLife Today*, covers a different topic. Then Christi leads a discussion with the women as they respond to what they've just heard. Between twenty and thirty women attend every year, and in a recent group, one-third of the women were single moms. With this particular group she adjusted the chapter on marriage and had a panel of two single moms and two married moms share. She has also invited seasoned empty-nester moms to come share their story. Christi relates, "Sharing this important season in this way has created a community of women who have come to love one another and minister to one another."

Christi's idea is not hard to copy. It takes initiative to think of others and to reach out to them at a time when many moms feel very lost. May some of you be inspired to do the same in your community!

### Event #3: An Empty-Nest Getaway

**Purpose:** An opportunity for an extended time away to reflect and celebrate. This would be a more in-depth time.

**Theme:** Sharing life stories and casting vision

**Guests:** These could be women that you know well and already have deep relationships with, or women who want to go deeper.

**Decor and Food:** Keep it simple. If you will be doing your own cooking, assign shopping and preparation to different people. You might have each woman bring a book that has been particularly meaningful to her for a book exchange.

**Program:** Take some extended time for each person to share. (You might use some of the reflection questions from the preceding chapter.) Take time to pray for each person after her time of personal sharing.

You might also consider inviting an older empty-nest woman to come and speak to your group. Even if she is not a trained speaker, having someone who is five to ten years ahead tell her story gives you and your friends a vision and hope.

Another idea is to make two lists as a group: (1) a list of all the positives of the empty nest and (2) a list of future "callings" that can make a difference in the lives of others. By doing this, you will focus on the positives and begin to spur one another to consider your next adventure.

Inject some lightness into your getaway (for example, old-movie night, makeovers and pedicures, hilarious skits, or dancing to the oldies). Think fun!

### Event Wrap-Up

Each event should provide an opportunity for women to share both their joys and their sorrows. Depending on how tender some are, it may be easier to focus on heartaches than move to the benefits. Sometimes we simply need a reminder of the blessings. Here are a few to start your thinking:

- less cooking
- lower water bills
- house stays clean longer
- no school calendars to dictate life
- midday lovemaking on the sofa
- no more worries about birth control or PMS
- a quiet home—no sibling rivalry within earshot
- your child's new independence (you're not in control anymore)
- hardly any trash to take out
- more time to hang out with girlfriends

When your party ends, you may wonder, *What now?* It's helpful to have several follow-up ideas in mind *before* your event. You may want to use your event as a kick-off to a short study on the empty nest. (See the four-session Small Group and Book Club Study Guide in the back of this book.) Or you may simply want to plan a reunion luncheon in a month. Perhaps there's one woman with whom you particularly identify. Invite her for coffee and get to know her story. You never know what God may have in mind for your future friendship.

SUSAN: One of the common longings each of us has is to be known and accepted. Years ago, I was on a retreat with a small group of women. Near the beginning of our time away, each woman took thirty minutes to share her story—her youth, her faith journey, the specific people who had impacted her along the way and how, etc. When one of the participants, a well-known, godly older woman, finished sharing her story, she looked at us in surprise and said, "You know something, no one has ever asked me to tell my story before. This has been so meaningful for me."

Whether it's dancing (like the Israelites did on the walls of Jerusalem), journaling your insights and dreams, going for a trip with your husband, or partying with girlfriends—however you choose to mark this transition—make it a celebration. You may be surprised with joy.

## Celebrate the Process of the Empty Nest

Celebrating the *process* might be the most difficult thing. Why? Because we want things tied up in neat packages. We long to have completion and closure. We like to check things off and move on to the next thing. But it's so hard to check off the empty nest. It really doesn't end; it merely has different phases. Throughout, there are times of both joy and grief—just like every other season of life.

It's easy to focus on the "next thing," to live with a *when/then* mentality: *When* I just get the kids out of the house, *then* . . . *When* we get a new house, *then* . . . *When* we get our finances settled, *then*. . . . But whenever you get *there*, you will simply find another *when/then*.

When we begin to view the empty nest not as something to rush through but as a season to enjoy, we will begin to appreciate the process. And we won't miss out on what God has to teach us *in* the process. For it is most often in the process that we learn life's most valuable lessons.

> The Lord is my strength and my shield; my heart trusts in him, and he helps me. My heart leaps for joy, and with my song I praise him.
>
> Psalm 28:7 NIV

# Take the Next Step

. . . . .

1. Make a list of all the positives you have discovered in the empty nest. Have your husband or a friend join in making this list and see how many you can think of.

2. Consider planning something to reaffirm your wedding vows. This could range from a special dinner for just the two of you to a more elaborate affair like a vow renewal ceremony.

3. What steps will you take to reconnect with some women? How can you spur one another to dream big about your next callings?

**Recommended Reading**

*The Radical Disciple: Some Neglected Aspects of Our Calling* by John Stott (InterVarsity Press, 2010)

# Tracy's Story

## Finally Used to Being Alone

Tracy began to feel the pangs of the empty nest when her daughter started her senior year. Because Tracy was a single parent and Monique was an only child, they had always been particularly close. "I called her my 'road dog,'" Tracy explained.

> We were always on the road together. Every morning before I went to work, I drove her thirty-five minutes to school, and at the end of each day I picked her up and we drove back home. Those times in the car were rich.
>
> I've always been involved in her life. I was the cool mom, and in her early teen years she was happy for me to be with her and her friends. But during her last couple of years in high school, she didn't seem to want me there as much. She wanted me to drop her off at the mall and leave. When she came home, she was more likely to go to her room and shut the door than talk. I sensed she wanted her space, and that gave me a bittersweet realization of what was to come.
>
> But the reality of it didn't hit me until I moved her into the dorm her freshman year. We had a blast decorating the room and hanging out with the girls in the hall. But then it was time for me to go. As I pulled out of the parking lot, with her face in my rearview mirror, I lost it. That face wasn't coming home tonight. It really was over.
>
> When I got home, the first thing that hit me was the silence. It was too quiet. I turned on every TV and radio in the house. And her once messy room was clean, too clean. It was eerie.

Tracy's husband had left them when Monique was nine. So for almost ten years, Tracy had been their sole provider through her job as an accountant. She had also been very involved in her church and in Bible Study Fellowship. She and her own mom were particularly close, and her mother had always been a positive role model.

> Nothing in my life has happened by chance. God has prepared me in every way, and I have learned to look for the blessings. Without the long school

drive in the morning, I have more time to sleep in. I can take time in the morning to pray and read my Bible.

God has shown me how to enjoy time alone with Him in a fresh way. I've learned to appreciate a different type of devotional time. My time with God is less likely to be interrupted by the phone ringing. Even though the house is quiet, I've begun to relish the peace.

She's also found time for long soaks in the tub, for digging in her garden, and even time to treat herself to pedicures. With less responsibility at home, she's taken on a new leadership role with Bible Study Fellowship's outreach to teenagers. She's continued to serve as a volunteer with Hawaiian Island Ministries, and she's begun to take business classes with the goal of starting her own event-planning company.

Most exciting of all, God has answered her prayer for a "man after God's own heart." Soon she will marry Donald; they met while watching their daughters play basketball. With the help of teammates, two girlfriends played matchmakers to introduce their single parents.

"I'd finally gotten used to being alone and liking it, and then God sends me a man," Tracy says with a laugh.

What has Tracy learned as she transitions through her empty nest to her next great adventure?

It's important to look back and see God's faithfulness. Nothing happens by chance. God always comes through, even at the eleventh hour. All those times I was afraid He wouldn't, He came through. He took care of me. Recognizing and remembering this enables me to take a risk in the future. He knows my faith is lacking as I move to a new marriage and a major career change. When I take time to remind myself of what He has done in the past, I have the courage to step out into the future.

# *Chapter* 11

# Discovering Your New Purpose

We waste our lives when we do not pray and think and
dream and plan and work toward magnifying God in
all spheres of life.

John Piper, *Don't Waste Your Life*

With the daily demands of motherhood behind you, it's time
to answer the question *What's next?*

In his letter to the church in Ephesus, Paul wrote, "For we are
His workmanship, created in Christ Jesus for good works, which
God prepared beforehand so that we would walk in them" (Ephesians 2:10). What a startling concept—God has unique tasks or
purposes for each of us that He prepared from the beginning of
time! Incredible.

How do we go about discovering our purpose?

Let's first agree that these purposes are NOT about sitting in
a rocking chair, idling our days away. As Kate Dewey said of the
boomer generation, "I think we're going to rewrite what retirement
means. . . . It's not going to be a passive experience."[1]

Judy Douglass, wife of the president of Campus Crusade for Christ International, makes a similar observation:

> Too many women define their lives only by raising children, so that when the kids leave home, these women feel their life's purpose is finished. They retire. They quit. They settle for trivial pursuits—in light of eternity—to occupy their time . . . but as long as we are on this earth, God has a great plan for our lives. He wants to use and leverage our maturity and experience for greater things in our second half of life.[2]

We agree. There is so much more we can do with our lives in this empty-nest season for the sake of others and for God's kingdom. There is indeed a next great adventure!

## Kay's New Purpose

Kay Warren is the wife of Rick Warren, who authored *The Purpose Driven Life*. In an interview recorded for *FamilyLife Today*, they shared how Kay discovered a new and unexpected purpose at the very start of her empty-nest season. We hope her story will inspire you to dream big.

> KAY: [God] changed my world in a flash one day. I was reading a news magazine, sitting in my living room in my nice, comfortable house, and read a news article on orphans in Africa. . . . I sat there and thought, *Do I even know a single orphan?* And the answer was, *No! Do I even know anybody who is HIV-positive? No.*
>
> To think that there could be 12 million children orphaned in one place due to one cause—it rocked my world. It became this intense internal dialog at first—*This just can't be true. I would know it if it were true.* And then it changed to, *Well, maybe if it's true, there's nothing I can do about it. That's too big. It's just too big for one person.*
>
> The plan that I had in place at that moment . . . was to travel around the world, be a Bible teacher, speak to pastors' wives and missionaries' wives. . . . So I thought that was just going to continue. And there's nothing wrong with that plan; it just wasn't God's plan. God had a completely different plan.

RICK: When she started sharing the vision, I said, "I'll support you in it. . . . It's not my vision, but I believe in what you're doing, and I'll support you."

KAY: And it grew from that acceptance and support. . . . I would bring videos and articles and say, "Read this, watch this, let's talk about that." . . . It just took a while to shift his focus, to realize that it wasn't just something that I was passionate about, but that he needed to also be passionate about it, and on top of that, our church needed to be passionate. . . . And not only did our church need to be passionate about it, but the church of Christ around the world needed to be passionate about it.

RICK: The lesson about this is . . . Husbands, listen to your wives. . . . They are in your life for a reason. God wanted to speak to me. He spoke to Kay first, and then He spoke through Kay to me, and it grabbed my heart. . . . The scales fell off my eyes, and I realized what a big deal this issue of orphans, and particularly those orphaned by AIDS, was.[3]

After visiting Africa to see firsthand the needs and the efforts of many who are working tirelessly to help, Rick stated, "I will give the rest of my life to guys like this who are working on the orphan issue and the AIDS issue and the poverty issue and the illiteracy issue and the things that are what we call *The Global Giants.*"[4] Global giants. Could God want you to help slay some of these massive challenges that threaten our world? Could it be that God wants you and your husband to be significant players in His agenda? Are you ready and willing to hear from Him?

It will take an army of men and women combining time and talents and treasures to bring about significant changes in our world. And we *have* an army. Millions of us empty nesters could become world changers. Each one of us can—and we believe *should*—seriously consider what God wants us to do.


### It's Time to Find Out!

What's next for *you* starts with identifying the unique experiences in the story of your life and the passions God has placed on your heart, then appraising your personal values, gifts, and talents. Some of you will enjoy the process and opportunity to explore, discover, and focus on finding your new purpose. Others of you may find an empty-nest vision slowly evolving as you continue with ongoing responsibilities.

As a mother, you probably made the development of your kids' talents a priority, and rightly so. But now you have the opportunity to evaluate your own uniqueness, including the spiritual gifts God has given you as a follower of Christ. The empty nest is ripe for self-discovery.

However you choose to proceed with our suggestions, understand that your journey of discovery needs to take place in the context of the important relationships in your life, especially with your husband, but also those including your children and perhaps even grandchildren, parents, and co-workers. We aren't suggesting that you ignore the people God has given you to love.

Remember also that the empty nest is a transition from one season and purpose to another. Just as many college students spend the first year or two deciding what their major will be, your journey of discovery will take some time as well. Be patient. But be assured, God has a plan.


### Get Ready . . . Get Set . . . Shop!

BARBARA: With Susan living in Virginia and me in Arkansas, much of the writing of this book was done with nearly nine hundred miles between us. Thankfully, though, we were able to spend a few days together now and then. One particular day, after several hours of working hard on the book, we decided that we had earned a break. I persuaded Susan to go shopping—no easy task, since she doesn't really enjoy shopping all that much.

What better way to get some exercise, we decided, than to walk around in an open-air mall! The weather was beautiful, so off we went. As we walked past shop windows, we couldn't miss a giant sale sign in one shoe store window, so we had to check it out. And there we spotted a pair of leopard print flats that we (Barbara and another friend) thought would be perfect for Susan. Though the reluctant shopper needed coaxing, we talked her into trying them on. They fit just right, and she bought them. She probably wouldn't have even considered the shoes if we hadn't suggested that she try them. Now she loves them!

In a similar way, we're going shopping with you, and we'll encourage you to try some things that you perhaps have never considered before. We're going to help you inventory what's in your closet—what you already have and what you might need. We'll be like a friend who says, "That would look great on you. You should try it!" Our desire is to serve you, to help you discover more of who you are and what God's purposes for you might be.

## What's in Your Closet? (Taking Your Inventory)

While we admit to making some impulse purchases—who hasn't?— the best way to begin any shopping adventure is to first check out our closets to see what we already have and what we need.

This is similar to the approach that we're going to recommend in the next several pages—to take inventory of your life before trying new things. You may choose to reverse the order and try new things first. That's fine. Ultimately the order doesn't matter. What does matter is that you approach this season with great intentionality. Four things to know will be helpful as you pull together your inventory.

### 1. Know Your Story

Begin by reflecting on your life story (as we suggested in chapter 9). The themes that have colored your life thus far are a significant part of figuring out God's next purpose. Like the foundation underneath a house, the personal journey that is behind you supports the purpose and mission that is before you.

There is an old poem that begins with these lines:

My life is but a weaving between my God and me.
I cannot choose the colors He worketh steadily.[5]

What colors has God worked into your life that He wants to use now? What have you always loved doing since you were a child? What gets your adrenaline flowing? What do you do to refuel when your emotional tank is empty?

Do your answers involve people or tasks? Creating or organizing? Doing or thinking? There are no right or wrong answers, yet there are themes that keep surfacing to bring color to your life. Ask God to guide you in seeing what He sees in you, to see what He has been weaving into your life. Discover who you are.

## 2. Know Who You Love

When we recognize the themes from our life story, we begin to understand the longings that God has planted in our hearts that He wants to continue to develop for the purpose of restoring more of our broken world.

BARBARA: My childhood dream of adoption—which became a reality in 1983 when we adopted a three-day-old baby girl—has been a bright thread in the fabric of my life. I love babies, and my heart has always been drawn to orphans and their sadness. As a result, adoption and orphan care will always be a part of my mission in some way. It is a part of my story, my individuality, and it reveals one of my passions.

SUSAN: When I look back over my life and reflect on the group of people I have been consistently the most passionate about, a common theme emerges—the next generation. John and I began our ministry working with junior and senior high school students. Then our kids came along. Later, as I graduated from diaper changing, my heart went out to younger mothers of babies. After our kids moved through the teen years, I felt compelled to encourage parents of teenagers. This passion continues today as I focus on young families. The funny thing is that I hadn't realized my continuing passion until we began this book and I looked back over my life to identify recurring themes.

From the themes of *your* life story will emerge those for whom you feel a tug of compassion. And this compassion will become the platform for expressing the heart of God to others.

As mothers, we wanted to make things right in the world for our children, even though we couldn't fix all that was broken. This is part of how God made us as women and as human beings. The desire for all things to be made right is the desire for perfection and, ultimately, for heaven and eternity—for all that is broken, tragic, unexplainable, or senseless to be made right. He who sits on the throne of heaven is the God of love, who has created us to be like Him, to be His hands and arms and feet of love. God is the Author of true passion and compassion.

What do you wish you could fix? What passion has He given you? What desires has He placed in your heart for His glory, knowing that you can do those particular things for Him? Who are the people, outside of your family, that God wants you to love—the homeless, the abused, the orphan, the poor, the elderly, the handicapped, those who have suffered through divorce, the children of divorce . . . ? Or perhaps your compassion is aroused when you hear of the suffering of widows, families affected by suicide, or teenage girls who need mentoring. Have you wondered if you had anything to offer women in crisis, children of single parents, college students, businesswomen, international students, or people from different ethnicities? Do you have a heart for evangelism, hospice care, AIDS work, or international slave trafficking victims? The pain in our world is endless, and God calls us to care for "the least of these" (Matthew 25:45) and to "overcome evil with good" (Romans 12:21). It's not optional, but a clear message to all who are believers.

Passion for others is what makes us feel alive, fulfilled, and significant.

189

To discover your personal passions, ask yourself some of these questions (start now while it is fresh on your heart). Then ask your husband or a friend who knows you well to give additional feedback.

- What would you change if you knew you couldn't fail?
- What cause would you champion if money and resources were unlimited?
- When do you most feel God's pleasure?
- What moves you most deeply?
- In what activity do you feel most alive?
- What causes or stories do you find yourself thinking about over and over again?
- What one specific need would you address that in your view would affect the most change in our world?

### 3. *Know Your Strengths*

When we truly consider the deep needs that so many people have, it would be easy to say, "But what do I have to offer?"

At a seminar I (Barbara) attended, I heard a speaker say that each individual possesses 100 to 150 strengths, talents, and abilities. That's an amazing figure! Can you believe that it's true of you?

Perhaps you feel that you have a good understanding of your personality and strengths. On the other hand, have you even considered all the factors that make you the unique individual that you are? We humans are complex, and there is always more we can know about how God has made us. So we challenge you to be courageous and to explore. You might discover greater significance in life—something new, something different that God has for you.

BARBARA: One of the best things I've done in recent years is to focus on personal development. Even though I'd done some of this previously, the focus of my energy was on developing as a parent and then helping my children achieve their potential. My ambition during those years was to serve them so that they might become all that they could.

As the last child left home, my turn came for serious personal development. In my season of rest after our youngest went to college, I began to find and take several personal assessments that gave me more information on what I valued, how I related to others, and what made me unique.

If your goal is like ours, to become all that God intended in every way possible that He might some day say, "Well done, good and faithful servant" (Matthew 25:21 NIV), then taking the time to understand the way God has wired you is essential. As our dear friend Mary Jenson says in her book *Taking Flight From the Empty Nest*, "The question has changed from 'How will *they* turn out?' to 'How will *I* turn out?'"[6]

In this section, our shopping excursion turns from knowing what is in our closet to trying on some new things. Read through the following list of tools and resources and pick one to try. It may be helpful for you and your husband to take one of the assessments together. Though this book focuses on your unique needs as a woman, processing through some of these together can strengthen your marriage. Many of these tools are invaluable in helping a husband and wife better understand each other and work together. The best scenario for you may be to find a purpose for your life that complements your husband's areas of interest. If he is approaching retirement, it would be wonderful to discover a mission you can share.

**Servants by Design (www.youruniquedesign.com):** This is an online personal-strengths assessment. After filling out the questionnaire, you'll receive a twelve-page report detailing how you have been wired by God (e.g., your viewpoint on life, your motivation, your best work situations, your significant abilities and interests, etc.). The results will give you a great depth of information. This profile is being widely used in the U.S. by churches and Christian organizations and is well worth the nominal fee.

191

**Leading From Your Strengths (www.leadingfromyourstrengths .com):** Once you access the website, you will be instructed how to purchase a code that unlocks the inventory. You are given the option of receiving your report immediately or having it emailed to you.

BARBARA: Dennis and I took this profile together, and it provided us with one of the most helpful pieces of information for our marriage in years. It was, in fact, revolutionary for us. Leading From Your Strengths plots your personal responses on four opposing scales: aggressive/passive, optimistic/realistic, fast-paced/slow-paced, and rules-follower/risk-taker. Each scale or quadrant has been named with an animal, which makes the results much more memorable and even humorous.

For Dennis and me, the greatest revelation came through the pace scale. He measured very high on the fast-paced scale, and I measured very high on the slow-paced scale. He was described as dynamic, hurried, intense, spontaneous, progressive, and excited. My descriptors were amiable, systematic, logical, patient, relaxed, and unhurried. Just the two words *hurried* and *unhurried* said it all! It suddenly made so much sense why we clashed over things, especially the schedules we keep and the way we like to keep them. It was well worth the price of the test for the benefit we have gained personally.

**The Significant Woman:** This seminar was developed by a team of women in Orlando in conjunction with others from around the U.S. and Australia. This seminar is thorough and walks a woman through the discovery of her strengths and weaknesses, her spiritual gifts, and her values and beliefs, with the outcome of writing a personal mission statement. To find a seminar in your area, visit www.significantwoman.com.

*Unlimited Partnership*: This book, written by Lloyd Reeb and Bill Wellons, might be especially helpful if you're interested in finding a role through your local church. The co-authors, a businessman and a pastor, discuss the way our vocational life can be used for ministry purposes. (B & H Books, 2007)

***Now, Discover Your Strengths***: This book, by Marcus Brotherton and Donald O. Clifton, features access to an online assessment tool (www.strengthsfinder.com). (FreePress, 2001)

**Spiritual gifts assessment:** If you have never taken one of these, we suggest you check with your church to see what they may have to offer. Many churches have classes and Bible studies available to help their members understand the concept of spiritual gifting. If your church does not have such a class or study, ask members of your church staff if they know of any assessments or books you might read. It's not hard to find content on this topic with a simple Internet search.

**Personal values assessment:** From shopping for clothes to choosing a lifelong career, values drive our decisions. What we value determines our behavior, our choices, and how and where we live. The Bible says, "For where your treasure is, there your heart will be also" (Matthew 6:21). Values determine choices, which reveal what our hearts treasure.

In the empty-nest season, we have the opportunity to objectively look at the values we have lived by to determine if what we have treasured has actually brought us fulfillment. We have an opportunity to realign our lives according to new values if we realize that the old ones were empty or misplaced, or if our ladder has been leaning against the wrong wall.

Narrowing the focus of your time and energy in God's direction can be accomplished by clearly identifying the values He has developed in your life over time. You can try some of the tools we have listed that offer values assessment components, or you can work through the simple exercise we've included in appendix 4.

Knowing your strengths will enable you to find a good fit for your time and energy and help you eliminate things that are not good matches. We urge you to take advantage of the evaluation tools that are so widely available.

### 4. Know What You Love to Do

BARBARA: When my daughters and I go shopping for clothes, we often say to one another, "Only buy what you love," and "Don't buy it unless it is an A-plus." Usually, we take several items into a dressing room and decide on only one; and many times, none. It's our way of eliminating all that is merely acceptable in favor of the best.

This is the approach to take as you digest this chapter. Look over all that has been offered. Decide what you'd like to try—we hope you will risk trying something new. Then, evaluate what you have discovered. Before leaving the dressing room, you have to decide what you love. What is the A-plus fit that you want to take with you?

Now, how will you pull it together with what you already have in your closet? That's the last step in the process of discovering your new purpose. Summarize who you are and those you love in relation to your strengths, values, and passions by writing your thoughts down on paper.

One way to do this is to write a personal mission statement. This isn't meant to be a stiff, impersonal statement that you quickly write, then save to your computer's hard drive or stuff in a desk drawer. Yes, we want you to write it down and keep it, but the statement should reflect *life*—your life. It should mean something to you in that it summarizes the journey God has you on and envisions where He's taking you next.

Mission statements are the norm for most corporations, businesses, ministries, and even schools. They grow out of discussions in which common values and goals emerge. A personal mission statement is no different. (And we suggest that you take this a step further by trying to formulate a mission statement or vision statement for your marriage, as we mentioned in chapter 5.)

A mission statement becomes your North Star, the direction of your new life purpose. A mission statement is what keeps you from saying yes to a host of activities that might be good but aren't best. A personal mission connects your uniqueness with God's purposes and ignites the hope that your life reaches beyond yourself. It channels your energy toward issues that really matter and burdens that God has placed on your heart. Likewise, a mission statement for your marriage can ignite your life as a couple with excitement and dreams that you haven't felt since the early days of your relationship. (You'll find examples at the end of chapter 12.)

We understand that the process of discovery and the risk of trying new things can be intimidating. But honestly, we have found it liberating. Our excitement builds as we discover how God has been preparing us for this new season and its many adventures. So we encourage you to start the journey for yourself. Don't take a job or sign up for a class or say yes to a task just because that's what your friend did or your workout partner said she'd recommend. Discover your new purpose by knowing your story, your passion, your strengths, and what God has given you a love for.

We want to lead lives that are transformed and renewed, not conformed to what everyone else is doing. And we want that for you, too.

> And do not be conformed to this world, but be transformed by the renewing of your mind, so that you may prove what the will of God is, that which is good and acceptable and perfect.
>
> Romans 12:2

# Take the Next Step

· · · · ·

Try one of the personal assessment tools suggested in the chapter.

## Recommended Reading

*Dangerous Surrender: What Happens When You Say Yes to God* by Kay Warren (Zondervan, 2007)

*When Invisible Children Sing* by Chi Cheng Huan and Irwin Tang (Tyndale, 2011)

# Elaine and Bob's Story

## Taking a Big Risk

From the time she was a little girl, Elaine had a heart for the people of the world. Later, while she and her future husband, Bob, were students at Wheaton College, they listened to some visiting speakers and were challenged to serve others, particularly those from other cultures.

As a young couple with three small children, they settled in Richmond, Virginia, where Bob practiced law and later served on the governor's staff. Elaine became involved in the inner city and in education. Frequently they opened their home to internationals and often felt that their calling was to give their church a bigger picture of what God was doing around the world. They struggled with the disproportion of Christian resources in the West while the greatest growth in the kingdom was in the non-Western world.

"We had lots of dinner parties at our home to which we'd invite people of different backgrounds and countries of origin," Elaine explains. "Our goal was to cross-pollinate Americans and internationals and expose our friends to new ways to serve God. We realized that as we encouraged others to serve God, we, too, were being challenged."

During their children's teen years, Elaine and Bob became the primary caregivers for both sets of parents and two other relatives. It was an intense season, but God was using it to train them in serving others with compassion.

By the time they reached their early fifties, the older adults under their care had died and their youngest child was ready to leave for college. They sensed a new freedom and a fresh possibility. But what would it look like? Elaine recalls,

We saw this open window, and we wanted to do something different for the next season in our lives. We didn't know where or what we were called to, but we wanted to find out. So we began a two-year period of intense research.

We benefited from extensive personal testing with Second Half Ministries [part of The Navigators at the time[7]]. We talked to people who knew us well and asked them how they had seen God use us. We wrote out our mission statements and asked God to show us where we could best serve Him.

During this process we realized that we had often been used to bring people together across denominational and regional lines. We loved internationals, and often used our home in serving them.

This was just the first phase. We followed up numerous possibilities that friends suggested. Often one contact led to another. Eventually, doors opened for a ministry to equip pastors in Asia, where the greatest need for the growing church is trained leaders.

Bob says,

This process was hard in many ways. It was difficult for me to think of leaving a steady income and raising my own salary. For me it was a one-step-at-a-time sort of faith walk. I'd read somewhere that if a man isn't thinking about a career change by age forty-five and making "trial probes" into the next possibility, by fifty he will be unlikely to risk it. So I took a trial probe by using vacation time to go on a short-term mission trip to Asia.

After seven years of living in Asia and encouraging emerging churches there, Elaine and Bob reflected on lessons learned. Bob says,

After doing all the research to make the decision, I realized I had to overcome inertia. I was still hesitant. Another man challenged me, "Just do it, Bob. It's a step of faith." He gave me the impetus at the right time to step out. As much as I wish they were, life's big decisions aren't always clear. Life is a walk of faith all the time.

Elaine adds,

We were two strong-willed people with different gifts wanting to complement each other. Working together 24/7 for the first time in our lives, we had to learn how to fit together in a new way. It was easier to identify who we were as individuals than to identify who we were as a couple. We're still learning! But in the learning, God has given us a greater dependency upon Him and a greater picture of what He's doing in the world today.

# Chapter 12

## Changing Your World

A man following Christ's teaching is like a man carrying a lantern before him at the end of a pole. The light
is ever before him, and ever impels him to follow it,
by continually lighting up fresh ground and attracting
him onward.

Leo Tolstoy

The first baby boomer turned sixty in 2006, and millions are
following close behind. And now the first Gen Xers are turning
fifty; many are or will be empty nesters soon. We believe that a great
percentage of women and men in their empty-nest years will have
the time, health, and resources to significantly impact the world if
we can be given a dream and a vision.

Just as an army of women in the United States and Great Britain
united their labor and sacrificed greatly in order to fuel, support, and
ensure the success of the Allied troops in World War II, so today,
in this season of our lives, women can unite in living second-season
lives of great purpose for the good of millions around the world.

You don't have to travel overseas to change the world. Those who make life better for foster children, single parents, the sick, and the elderly are world changers (as our friends have illustrated in these pages). Jesus said, "As you did it to one of the least of these my brothers, you did it to me" (Matthew 25:40 ESV). Real passion is always about helping others, which in turn changes the world. "If our deepest dreams aren't about other people, then we have settled for mere power and accomplishment," writes Dan Allender.[1]

Known only to a few people, Sue, Sally, and Jackie are helping to change their world. Their lives were already full with elder care, children's weddings, grandbaby arrivals, and husbands to support in new jobs and retirement. Friends for over thirty years, these three had been there for one another through the loss of a child, a teenager's rebellion, a husband's stroke, and lots of other challenges. And they'd shared the joys as well—the return of the prodigal, the blessing of a grandchild coming to faith, and the richness of years of knowing and being known.

These three friends have had a long-standing routine. Early in the morning they meet at a designated street corner for their fast-paced walk up the long hill through their small town. Then an hour later, sweaty and exhausted, they head for their reward—coffee at the local Starbucks.

One particular morning seemed like any other . . . until they noticed a younger mom standing in line for coffee and invited her to sit with them.

"How's it going?" Sue asked, sensing that she was heavyhearted.

The young woman burst into tears. "I'm having such a hard time with my teenage daughter," she unloaded. "I just don't know what to do."

For the next half hour, Sue, Sally, and Jackie shared their own experiences—what they had done wrong themselves, what had worked well, and what they had learned. They comforted and they gave advice.

As the younger mom got up to leave, she exclaimed, "Oh my. Thank you so much. Now I have hope."

Sally was quick to reply, "Well, it's just free advice. You can take it or leave it." Then and there the Take It or Leave It club was born.

Since that day, many women have sought these three out at the coffee shop. New friendships have formed, advice has been given and received, and older women have prayed for younger women.

When a group of women in another state learned about the Take It or Leave It club, they immediately wanted something like this for themselves. They approached several older women in their community with an idea of opening up a front porch once a week for a Take It or Leave It time. In another city, women started meeting at a local playground.

What is happening here? A natural form of mentoring. One of the most repeated requests that the two of us have heard is from younger women longing for older women to whom they can go for advice. This is a distinctive trait of this younger generation. We baby boomers weren't inclined to go to older women for advice, but the next generation is!

What our friends have done is simply make themselves available. They have intentionally reached out in friendship to younger women whom they don't necessarily know. They've offered a listening ear, shared their own failures and successes, given biblically based advice, and prayed for each woman.

Some will find their calling to big issues—what the world terms "significant endeavors." This is good. On the other hand, God may be calling you to reach out to the younger women in your community, which is equally valid and good. We believe He wants each of us to be a "FAT" woman—Faithful, Available, and Teachable.

So begin to dream about what *you* can do to change lives, to make the world a better, safer place for one or for many.

Paul David Tripp writes in his excellent book *Lost in the Middle*,

> Imagination is not conjuring up what is unreal, but what is real, only unseen. God hardwired us with the ability to "see" what cannot be seen, to commune with one with whom we cannot physically converse, to love the one whom we cannot touch. We human beings are

wired to dream. It is what gives us station and dignity among the rest of creation. This ability to imagine is wonderful, mysterious, practical, holy, mundane and amazing. It is particularly significant for believers because we accept the fact that there is a God who really does exist, who cannot be seen, touched or heard.[2]

In 1963, Martin Luther King Jr. gave his famous "I Have a Dream" speech that has inspired millions in the decades since. We, too, have a dream. Ours is to see this generation of empty-nest women, especially Christian women, change the world. Just as God used the advances of the Roman Empire for the rapid spreading of the gospel of Christ in the first few hundred years after the resurrection, could He not also use us and the technology of the present day to bring truth and hope and help to millions around the world?

We women know how to give our lives for others. We've been doing it for years. Now is the time to find a new focus for those well-seasoned abilities and talents God has built into us.

The two of us long to go deeper, and we want our lives to count for things that really matter.

- Will you join us as we continue to discover what God has for each of us individually?

- Will you search for the course that God has set before you and run with endurance the rest of your life for Him?

- Will you vow to use the ability and energy God has given you to rebuild the ruined lives around you, to be a voice for those who have no voice, to pray for those who have no one to intercede for them, to join others in the hard work of rescuing men, women, and children in need?

C. T. Studd once wrote, "Only one life, 'twill soon be past, Only what's done for Christ will last!"[3]

> If you extend your soul to the hungry and satisfy the
> afflicted soul, then your light shall dawn in the darkness,

and your darkness shall be as the noonday. The Lord will guide you continually, and satisfy your soul in drought, and strengthen your bones; you shall be like a watered garden, and like a spring of water, whose waters do not fail. Those from among you shall build the old waste places; you shall raise up the foundations of many generations; and you shall be called the Repairer of the Breach, the Restorer of Streets to Dwell In.

Isaiah 58:10–12 NKJV

# Take the Next Step

1. Write a personal mission statement.

   A personal mission statement is simply a sentence that states your purpose in life—what you are about as a person. It's a clarifying declaration reminding yourself why you are here on earth. A mission statement can change and become more focused as we get older and more mature. In the movie *Chariots of Fire* (1981), Eric Liddell made this statement about his running: "I believe God made me for a purpose, but he also made me fast. And when I run I feel His pleasure."[4] When do you feel the pleasure of God? When have you sensed, *I was made for this?*

   When you are ready to seriously tackle this, begin by summarizing all you have learned about yourself from the exercises suggested in chapter 11 into these four topic statements:

   My life themes and passions are:
   My top values are:

My spiritual gifts are:
My personality and personal strengths are:

Work to refine this into a short statement or two. For example, Claire wrote that her mission is "to use my gifts, talents, and personality in the marketplace to teach and encourage women to have a meaningful relationship with Jesus." Another friend, Carol, wrote, "My mission is teaching women to apply biblical principles for the purpose of approaching life with an eternal perspective."

Next, evaluate the causes where you might invest your time and energy. Remember that a mission statement reflects the passion God has put on your heart. Then, you need to determine whom you want to invest in and how you can use your life, talents, and gifts to help them.

2. Write a marriage mission statement.

The spark for this idea came from Susan's son Chris and his new bride, Christy, who wrote a marriage vision statement on their honeymoon. We liked the idea as a way for us older couples to redirect our marriages toward the finish line with renewed purpose and vision.

We asked several dozen empty-nest couples to craft a marriage mission statement, and we got a wide variety of responses. One woman wrote, "I can see how it would be easy for us to just move on to separate activities in the empty nest. So now I'm thinking, 'As a couple what is our uniqueness? What are our top five values? What are we passionate about together?' And it's been good for us to talk about this."

Gary and Cindy approached their mission statement in a unique way by looking at older people. They listed traits and themes they wanted to emulate in three key areas:

**Attitude** (based on Philippians 4:8):
• To make our home safe, welcoming, and fun
• To listen well

- To share wisdom and advice when we've been given permission
- To be patient and not demanding
- To be willing to take risks, make mistakes, try new things
- To remain technologically savvy
- To remain culturally relevant, so we can communicate with the next generation

**Serving others** (based on Philippians 2:4):
- To be focused on others, not self-focused
- To be involved in the lives of our children and grandchildren
  For example, Cindy's mom did a great job of building long-distance relationships with her grandchildren. They had "girls week" and "boys week" at their grandparents' house every summer, giving them a chance to build into the lives of the grandchildren while the kids developed relationships with their cousins.

**Finishing well** (based on Deuteronomy 34:7):
- To diligently take care of our health
- To not become complacent about our physical intimacy, but to remain vibrant into old age
- To remain well read and to stay on the cutting edge of culture and Christianity
- To fight the good fight, to finish well
- To die well, strong in faith to our last breath

## Recommended Reading

*Embracing Your Second Calling: Find Passion and Purpose for the Rest of Your Life* by Dale Hanson Bourke (Thomas Nelson, 2010)

# *Epilogue*

## Barbara and Susan Today

**F**our years after our first conversation about the empty nest, we finished the first edition of this book. Since then we've continued to talk about how our marriages continue to grow and change, and how we relate to our adult children and their families, because it's not always easy. And now we are finishing an updated version for a new generation of empty-nest women.

And we continue to learn a lot from each other and from many other women along the way. It's been good for each of us, this journey into the empty nest. Both of us have grown in our relationships with God, with our husbands, and with our adult kids. We've been reminded over and over that the empty nest is an ongoing adventure. We're still learning.

BARBARA: Because my personality is inclined toward details and planning, I initially worked through many of the tools and read most of the books we recommended in chapters 9 and 11. Though a clear, concise personal mission statement has eluded me, I have instead started a new venture within FamilyLife, a holiday and home collection called Ever Thine Home. The byline I worked on for months and finally felt was right is "Believe beautifully." Those two words are not a mission statement in the true sense of the word, but they do sum up who I am and what I love. And the work of creating beautiful Christmas ornaments and other Christ-honoring items for women has become my new mission in the empty nest. It's now a full-time job; I've learned so much, and it's been a good use of the gifts God has built in me. You can find out more at everthinehome.com.

One of the many lessons I've learned from Susan is that transitions in life are normal and constant. As empty nesters, my husband and I are, and will continually be, in transition because of aging and changing family dynamics. We've discovered, as a result, a greater opportunity to intentionally work on our marriage relationship. It's been gratifying and meaningful to dig deeper in communication, to plan fun adventures like we did when we were first married, and to dream together about the impact we want to have on the world before we leave it. We love our marriage today and wouldn't go back to the early days even if we could.

SUSAN: Looking back, I realize that I fell headlong into the empty nest with little forethought. When it hit me, no one was talking about this season. There were few models and there was very little help for those of us in this transition. I did not take any tests or do any detailed planning. I just *kept on going.* And life just kept getting more complicated. Most often I swept aside my feelings and simply dove into the next thing. Overly responsible and driven by nature, it has been hard for me to rest.

Barbara has helped me to refocus on my need for Sabbath rest. I've realized in a fresh way how crucial it is to take time to *let my soul catch up with my body,* and to do so without feeling guilty. After all, it's a commandment! Even though we've been empty nesters for a number of years now, John and I find it helpful each August to look at the upcoming year and ask ourselves several questions: What changes do we need to make? How can we be more intentional in resting, in taking time for the two of us, and spending time with our kids and grandkids while still juggling demanding schedules? It's not easy. And I know it will always be an evolving process.

The good news is that God is *in* the process, and throughout life we have discovered that He's more interested in the process than in the results. We live in a world that applauds accomplishment, completion, and closure. But God values simple day-in, day-out relinquishment and trust. Frustrating as it may be, this empty nest is not a season we finish.

As Barbara and I look to the future, our goal is to make the most of the years we have left. We long to grow in relationship with God, with our family members, and with our friends—including each other. We want to work diligently to maintain our health and energy, and to impact as many people for good as we can, encouraging them to use their gifts to make a positive difference in the lives of others.

We long to be positive, grateful women who age with grace. This requires intentionally choosing—on a daily basis—to trust God with whatever He brings and to always give thanks. Aging well doesn't just happen. Being productive with our gifts and talents and making a significant difference in the lives of others doesn't happen easily. It takes courage and hard work to counteract the far easier drift into self-centeredness and shallow thinking.

In the process of writing this book together, we've been given many gifts, the most precious one being that of our friendship. We've learned how different we are and yet how similar we are. We've been pushed to deeper levels of vulnerability and found challenge and comfort in each other. We've experienced fear, frustration, sweat, laughter, relief, and downright amazement at God's faithfulness. If no one else reads this book, we are grateful to Him for the gift He's given us—a friend to walk alongside.

Even though an epilogue is supposed to mark the end of a story, we feel instead that we are actually at the beginning of a new chapter. Our journey into the next adventure is barely under way. We invite you to visit both of our blogs: Susan's at susanalexanderyates.com and Barbara's at everthinehome.com. We'd love to be in touch with you. God is writing a new chapter in your life, too, and we'd love for you to share it with us.

# Helpful Hints for Caring for Your Parents and In-laws As They Age

As you care for your parents and in-laws, be sure to assess these three areas:

## Housing and Logistics

1. Is their living situation adequate? Is it necessary to add conveniences or services (e.g., yard work, maintenance, housekeeping, driving substitutes) to allow parents to age in their current place?

2. Is their home adaptable for future years (e.g., first-floor bedroom and bath or accessibility from the outside without steps)?

3. What are their wishes about housing and care should they become incapacitated? Have they considered the local options or looked at any continuing care communities?

4. Is there a need for assistance or simplification regarding grocery shopping and meals? Consider Meals on Wheels, individual frozen dinners, microwave meals, a grocery delivery service, or other creative support systems to allow elderly parents to stay independent.

5. Is it still safe for them to drive? A family doctor may be able to help decide.


## Financial and Legal

Each state has its own laws on wills, power of attorney, living wills, health care, etc. It is important that these documents be reviewed by a lawyer in the state where your parents reside.

1. Are they managing their finances adequately? Can you help with writing checks, arranging automatic deposits, or having their bills sent to you instead of them? In order to safeguard your parents from confusion or scam artists, it might be wise to have duplicate financial statements—including bank statements, credit card statements, and broker statements—sent to you so that you can monitor them monthly. This allows your parents to write their own checks, and it allows you to protect them as you monitor their financial situation.

2. Is there an inventory of assets, including insurance policies and retirement plans? Is property held jointly with others? It is very important to consider whose name their property is in. It may need to be changed. Who are the beneficiaries on the policies?

3. Is there a living will? Who has the power to make health care decisions? Their primary care doctor and or hospital should have copies of health care powers of attorney and/or living wills and advance directives depending on the state's requirements.

4. Have they had legal counsel in drawing up an estate plan? This document should be reviewed if there are changes in the size of the estate or the desires of your parents. It is helpful to review the document every couple of years with a lawyer who practices in the area of estate planning.

5. Are essential documents prepared and available as needed? These documents should include durable, general power of attorney; advance directives for health care; and a will.

6. Does someone know the location of their safety deposit box? It is wise for someone other than the parents to be on the signature card. Do they have documents stored in other places?

Here is a short list of documents and information you should have for your parents (and your children should have for you):

1. Location of original will
2. Names and contact information of lawyers, advisers, and brokers
3. Name and contact information of the person with power of attorney

## Spiritual

While we prepare financially and legally for the end of life, it's even more important to prepare spiritually. Take the opportunity to share with your parents how much God loves them. Give them specific passages from Scripture. Review the basics of a personal relationship with Christ, including His forgiveness and the assurance of eternal life with Him, which we have as believers.

# Helpful Hints for Growing in a Relationship With Christ

### Finding Certainty

There aren't many things that we can be certain of in this life. Much of life is a matter of faith.

One thing is certain, God will not lie. He has promised that if we ask Him to come into our life, He will. We are likely to have many questions, and there will be much we don't understand, especially in the beginning. But no matter what our background—what we have done or not done—God longs for each of us to come to Him. He wants us to have the certainty of knowing Him personally, not simply a vague hope that He exists.

If you aren't sure that you've ever asked Christ into your life and you would like to, please don't wait any longer. Here is a prayer similar to the one that each of us prayed when we asked Christ to come into our lives. We encourage you to pray this prayer for yourself and invite Christ into your life. You can trust Him to answer questions and to bring understanding as you begin to grow in Him.

*Dear Lord Jesus, I need you. I invite you into my life to be my Lord and Savior. Thank you for dying on the cross for me. Thank you that this painful act of yours has allowed my sins to be forgiven. Thank you that you have promised that you will never leave me. Thank you that I can know right now that one day I'll be in heaven with you, not because I'm good or bad, but because I'm forgiven.*

When you ask Christ into your life to be your Lord and Savior, several things happen.

**1. He comes in!** You may or may not have experienced strong feelings when you prayed. If you did, that's wonderful. But if you didn't, don't worry. Feelings or lack of feelings don't determine the authenticity of Christ coming into your life. He comes in response to being asked. A relationship with Him is not based on feelings. (What a relief!) It is based on faith in the fact that He will do what He has promised. See Revelation 3:20 and Titus 1:2.

**2. He will never leave you.** He promises that even when you forget Him or mess up, He will never leave you. See Hebrews 13:5 and Psalm 139:7–10.

**3. All your sins are forgiven.** When you ask God to forgive your sins, He does. Yes, even that one you can barely admit. He has forgiven that one, too. And He stands ready to forgive your future sins when you mess up. All you need to do is confess them and ask for His forgiveness. See 1 John 1:9 and Psalm 103:12.

**4. You can know that one day you will be in heaven with Him.** Going to heaven isn't dependent on being good. You could never be good enough. No one can. It is dependent on Christ taking on your sins when He died on the cross. See 1 John 5:11–12.

**5. He has given you His Holy Spirit to give you the power to live the life He has planned for you to live.** It isn't up to you to tough it out. Instead, He's given you the full power of the Holy Spirit to enable you to become the person He has created you to be. You can't do it alone. That is not His intention. His intention is that you become more and more dependent upon Him. When you depend on His Holy Spirit, you will experience His supernatural power and freedom. See John 14:26 and 16:13 and Ephesians 1:13–14.

**6. You have a new family of brothers and sisters in Christ who will help you grow in Him.** Just as our children go through different physical growth stages, you will go through different stages in your spiritual growth. You will need friends to whom you can go with your spiritual questions. No question, doubt, or feeling is silly or insignificant. You will be helped by having others who have been there to guide the way. We encourage you to seek out a church where the teachings are based on Scripture and to find a small group in which to be involved for encouragement. See 1 John 1:1–4 and 1 Thessalonians 5:11.

No longer do you have to *think* or *hope* or *wonder* if you are a believer. Now you are a *know-so* believer. You *know so* because God promised He would come into your life if you asked Him to. And God keeps His promises.

Another thing you can know is that you can approach Him with confidence. The Bible says, "In him [Jesus] and through faith in him we may approach God with freedom and confidence" (Ephesians 3:12 NIV).

You can approach God with every fear, concern, and confusion you have. Nothing is too silly. Nothing will shock Him. Nothing is too difficult for Him to handle. He longs for you to come to Him and to share your heart with Him just as you long for your kids to confide in you. He loves you even more than you love your children, so just imagine how much it thrills Him when you come to Him.

Our prayer is that your heart will be touched in a deep way with a fresh glimpse of how much your heavenly Father loves you.

# A Daily Focus
# on the Character of God

One of the lessons we continue to learn is how important it is *to focus on who God is rather than on who we are or are not.* It's so easy for our problems, issues, and fears to seem larger than God is. There's a wonderful promise in the Gospel of John that describes one of the functions of the Holy Spirit—to remind us of all that Christ has taught us.

> The Advocate, the Holy Spirit, whom the Father will send in my name, will teach you all things and will remind you of everything I have said to you.
>
> John 14:26 NIV

We find that it is helpful to ask the Holy Spirit to remind us daily of one of God's character traits. Then we try to reflect on this trait throughout the day.

We have included thirty-one days of character traits—one for each day of the month—for you to reflect on as you walk through this time of transition.

**Thank you that you are a God who . . .**

1. **Rescues**—You long to rescue me, my relative, my child, my friend (Psalm 18:19; 91:14–16).

2. **Delights in me**—At this moment you are delighting in me (Psalm 35:27; Zephaniah 3:17).

3. **Goes before**—You are going before me and my child to prepare the way (Ephesians 4:12; Psalm 48:14).

4. **Is in charge**—When it seems everything is falling apart, I can count on the fact that you are still in charge (Psalm 75:3; 103:19).

5. **Lavishes**—You are lavishing your love on me! (Ephesians 1:8; Psalm 145:7).

6. **Knows all**—You know everything about me. You know me better than I know myself and you love me (Psalm 139).

7. **Speaks**—You do speak in your time, in your way. You demonstrate this in creation! (Psalm 25:14).

8. **Understands**—When no one else can, you do—completely! (Psalm 139; 147:5).

9. **Is present**—Your presence is with me. You never leave me. You are a "with me" God (Exodus 33:14; Psalm 34:18).

10. **Is light**—Even if there is darkness around, there is no darkness in you (1 John 1:5; Psalm 27).

11. **Always forgives**—Even when I can't forgive myself or others, you do and you enable me to (Psalm 86:5; 1 John 1:9).

12. **Creates new things**—You never get stale. You are always doing something new (Ephesians 4:24; Ezekiel 36:26).

13. **Is always working**—Even when I can't see it, you are working while I'm waiting (Psalm 103).

14. **Fills**—Lord, I'm empty. Please fill me today with your Holy Spirit (Ephesians 1:23; 5:18).

15. **Exerts power**—You are working in my life with the same power that raised a man from the dead (Ephesians 1:19–20).

16. **Holds**—You are holding your child by your right hand and sustaining her (Psalm 55:22).

17. **Covers**—You are covering me today (Psalm 91:4).

18. **Provides**—You are providing in ways I don't even know, and you will provide in the future (1 Timothy 6:17).

19. **Is faithful**—I can always depend on you. You always come through (1 Corinthians 1:9).

20. **Is so much more**—You are so much more and will do so much more than I can imagine (Ephesians 3:20–21; Hebrews 11:40).

21. **Delivers**—You will deliver me, my child, my friend (Psalm 34).

22. **Shows unfailing kindness**—You are caring about my concern at this very moment (Psalm 18:50; 106:7).

23. **Is revealing**—You will reveal your will in your time (Proverbs 3:5–7; Psalm 90:17).

24. **Equips**—You are equipping me for what you have called me to do (1 Thessalonians 5:24).

25. **Pours out love**—Your love isn't parceled out, it's poured out! (Psalm 13:5; 130:7).

26. **Hears**—You do hear me—always! (Psalm 31:21–22; 116:1–2).

27. **Protects**—You are a "watching over me" God! (Psalm 121).

28. **Comforts**—You supernaturally console those who hurt (2 Corinthians 1:3–5; Psalm 94:19).

29. **Advocates**—You are my lawyer, my defender (Jeremiah 50:34).

30. **Brings out to a place of abundance**—You will refresh your children! (Psalm 66:12; 31:7–8).

31. **Intercedes**—Right at this moment you, Jesus, are praying for me (Hebrews 7:25; Romans 8:34).

# Values Assessment Exercise

To assess your values, start by listing them broadly (e.g., truth, compassion, adventure, etc.). Next, shorten your list by combining those that are similar. Then pare your list down to your top ten. Once you've done that, try to pare your list down to your top five. Base your decisions on values that you absolutely cannot give up. Consider inviting your husband to do the same, and merge your lists into one common list. Knowing what you value as a couple can be pivotal in making decisions and strengthening your marriage.

| | | |
|---|---|---|
| Accomplishment | Community | Duty |
| Adventure | Compassion | Education |
| Authenticity | Competence | Efficiency |
| Beauty | Contribution | Elegance |
| Biblical truth | Creativity | Empowerment |
| Career | Development | Encouragement |
| Changing the | of talents | Environment |
| world | Diligence | Equality |
| Children | Diversity | Excellence |

| | | |
|---|---|---|
| Fairness | Influence | Relaxation |
| Faith | Integrity | Risk taking |
| Faithfulness | Joy | Security |
| Family | Justice | Self-esteem |
| Finances | Learning | Self-expression |
| Forgiveness | Love | Sensitivity |
| Free time | Marriage | Service |
| Freedom | Mentoring | Sexual fulfillment |
| Friends | Mercy | Solitude |
| Frugality | Ministry | Spiritual growth |
| Fulfillment | Obedience | Spouse |
| Fun | Orderliness | Stability |
| Generosity | Passion | Stewardship |
| Gentleness | Patience | Success |
| Growth | Peace | Temperance |
| Happiness | Performance | Tolerance |
| Hard work | Perseverance | Tongue control |
| Health | Personal power | Tranquility |
| Heritage | Philanthropy | Trust |
| Honesty | Prestige | Truth |
| Honor | Productivity | Vision |
| Human dignity | Purity | Wealth |
| Humility | Purpose | Winning |
| Humor | Quality | Work |
| Identity | Recognition | Worship |
| Independence | Relationships | |

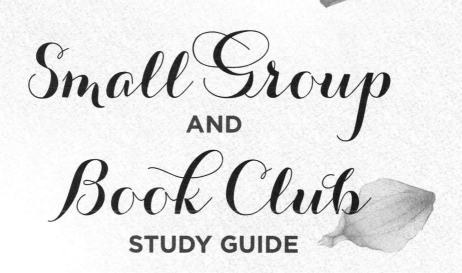

# Small Group
## AND
# Book Club
## STUDY GUIDE

# Introduction

We're glad that you are interested in leading a group study on the empty nest. One of our hopes is that by discussing this season we can build a new community of empty nesters who are willing to be honest about the challenges they face and who yearn to discover their next great adventure. Both of us have found it extremely helpful to have friends with whom we can share our fears and friends who will give us feedback as we dream about new ways to invest our time, recognize our unique gifts, and make a difference in the lives of others.

We'd like to learn from you, too, so please keep in touch with us through our blogs (everthinehome.com and susanalexanderyates .com) as your group progresses.

*Barbara Rainey & Susan Yates*

## Getting Started

If leading a group is a new experience for you, here are some suggestions to help you get started.

- Consider hosting or co-hosting one of the parties described in chapter 10. At your party present the idea of a book club and invite the women to sign up. It's best if you set the date for the first meeting (and preferably all of them) before the end of the party. Go ahead and give out the books at the end of the party to those who plan to participate.

- Pray that God will draw women to the study who will be able to gain the most from it. Don't hesitate to extend personal invitations to those God puts on your heart. Encourage the women at your party to invite others to attend, as well.

- Be realistic about the size of your group; eight to fifteen women is probably a good number to include, although a larger size can work. It is helpful to have two women facilitating the group.

- You might ask women in various stages of the empty nest— those approaching it, those in their first two or three years of it, and those who have been empty nesters for several years.

- Be sure that those who are planning to participate in your group get the book in time to read the first three chapters prior to the first meeting. If you hosted a party, these women will have received their book. As others are invited, have a friend deliver the book to them prior to the first meeting.

- Welcome diversity in your group. Some may be experienced believers who are familiar with the Bible and are intentional about living on the basis of scriptural principles, while others may not have a personal relationship with Christ. In fact, we hope many will use this book to reach out to neighbors and friends who are exploring matters of faith. The common challenges of this season can become a bridge to spiritual discussions.

- Be sensitive to the needs of those in your group. Some members will be willing to share very openly, while others may need time to build trust and to speak up. Be gentle, loving, and flexible. Most important, pray for your group members and try to keep in touch with them outside the group if possible.

- As the group leader, you will set the pattern for openness, honesty, and trustworthiness.

- Remind your group of the importance of speaking respectfully of spouses, parents, and children when talking about them in your discussion times.

- Use the suggested questions to help your group talk openly about their response to the book, but don't be bound by these questions. You may come up with other questions and ideas that will be even more suitable for your group. Flexibility will be key!

- Your group will gain much more in their discussion if the individuals have taken the time to read the chapters in advance. Also encourage group members to record their responses to the Take the Next Step sections that appear at the end of each chapter.

- Finally, remember that the purpose of your group is to provide encouragement. Do all you can to provide a safe environment where women can be honest about their challenges, worries, hopes, and fresh discoveries.

# Session One

## Chapters 1–3

### Get to Know One Another

At your first get-together, go around and have everyone share their names, professions, kids' ages, and where they are in the empty-nest process. You could ask them to share a challenge they have experienced and a blessing they have discovered.

### Warm Up

1. What has caused you to want to read a book about the empty nest?

2. What do you hope to gain through being a part of this discussion group?

### Talk It Over

3. Barbara tells the story of thinking that her mother was old—at the age of thirty-two!—because she couldn't remember her age

when the policeman asked. As a child, what things did you associate with old age?

4. What seems old to you now in terms of behavior?

5. *Empty nest* refers both to a season of life and a transition. Why is change often difficult for us to handle?

6. How has God used transitions in your life to draw you closer to Him or to mature you emotionally and spiritually?

7. What challenges do you anticipate as you move into the empty-nest season? What do you look forward to?

8. Of the many emotions experienced by empty nesters or soon-to-be empty nesters, loneliness seems to be universal. What help can we find for our loneliness through

- friends?
- family?
- God?

## Take It With You

Loneliness often comes as a result of some significant change in life. As we attempt to adjust, we often feel alone in the struggle, as if no one else could understand or empathize with us. This is why we are encouraged to, above all things, *run to God*. Read the following verses and explain what they teach us about the wisdom of running to God when we are struggling. Or share with the group other Bible passages that you have found helpful during these times.

> Therefore he had to be made like his brothers in every respect, so that he might become a merciful and faithful high priest in the service of God, to make propitiation for the sins of the people. For because

he himself has suffered when tempted, he is able to help those who are being tempted. . . .

Since then we have a great high priest who has passed through the heavens, Jesus, the Son of God, let us hold fast our confession. For we do not have a high priest who is unable to sympathize with our weaknesses, but one who in every respect has been tempted as we are, yet without sin. Let us then with confidence draw near to the throne of grace, that we may receive mercy and find grace to help in time of need.

Hebrews 2:17–18; 4:14–15 ESV

## Pray Together

As you close your time together in prayer, ask God to

- make your group a safe, encouraging, and helpful place for all who come;
- help each of you process the challenges of transition;
- guard your hearts from loneliness and isolation.

# Session Two

## Chapters 4-6

**Warm Up**

1. Now that you have the opportunity to talk about it with friends, are you starting to think differently about the empty-nest season? What are you thinking or feeling now that you hadn't before?

2. Barbara and Susan write about the importance of giving thanks. What are some people or things in your life that you are thankful for today?

**Talk It Over**

3. Describe what you think it means to "give thanks in all circumstances" (1 Thessalonians 5:18 ESV).

4. Barbara and Susan write about what they both learned through disappointing circumstances: "We cannot change the past, but we can control how we respond to it in the present." What advice would

you give to a friend who was having a hard time getting free from hurts of her past?

5. Do you agree with the statement "Usually, this season is harder on women than men"? Explain your answer.

6. Married couples were challenged to consider: "What is God calling us to do together that will make a positive difference in the lives of others?" Can you think of a couple who exemplifies this kind of life, who are giving their empty-nest years to serving others? Tell the group about them.

7. Describe what it means to be a helicopter parent. Describe what it means to be a hands-off parent. Which do you think you tend to be? What about your husband?

At the end of chapter 5, you were encouraged to write down two specific steps that you would take, along with your husband, to achieve more balance. If you can, please share your steps with the group.

8. Did it go well between you and your parents when you left home? What did you learn then that can be helpful to you now?

9. If you have adult children, how would you describe the nature of your relationship with them now? How is that relationship different from what it was when the child still lived at home?


**Take It With You**

Third John 4 reads:

> I have no greater joy than to hear that my children are walking in the truth. (ESV)

John was referring to his "spiritual" children—those whose spiritual development he had participated in. What would bring you the greatest joy regarding your "physical" children?

**Pray Together**

As you close your time together in prayer, focus on

- praying for one another as you deal with disappointments that could be making this season of transition even more difficult;
- praying for each other's marriages, that they would grow even stronger in the empty-nest years;
- praying for your children in five areas: spiritual, emotional, physical, mental, and social. (Perhaps refer to your prayer lists from the second assignment in the Take the Next Step section at the end of chapter 6.)

# Session Three

### Chapters 7–9

**Warm Up**

1. Did you have a favorite grandparent, aunt, or uncle? What was special to you about that relationship?

2. How would you like to be thought of by your nieces, nephews, and grandchildren? Describe the relationship you want with your sons-in-law or daughters-in-law.

**Talk It Over**

3. Keeping relationships free of regrets is a good goal, even though not always possible. Choose one of your key family relationships (children, in-laws, parents) and explain what you can do to keep that relationship regret free.

4. Does having an empty nest make it easier or more challenging for you to deepen (or repair) relationships with family members? Explain your answer.

5. Barbara and Susan offered several suggestions for strengthening family ties. What plans have you made, or are you considering, that could help your extended family connect more than they already do?

6. Chapter 8 opened with a list of questions that many women may be asking themselves as they enter the empty-nest season: *Who have I become? What is my purpose now that my kids are gone? Does anyone need me? How do I know what to do next? What am I good at? Where do I start?* Which of these questions are you personally dealing with at this moment? Or what other questions are in your thoughts?

7. What has and has not helped you get answers to these questions?

8. Some people seem to react negatively to the suggestion of taking a break. Why do you think they respond that way?

9. What do you like to do to rest and to be refreshed?

**Take It With You**

In several places, the Bible encourages us to talk to one another about the goodness of God and how we have personally experienced His goodness. One such place is Psalm 34:3:

> O magnify the Lord with me, and let us exalt His name together.

Psalm 78:4 calls one generation to tell the next generation about the things they have seen God do.

> We will not hide them from their children, but tell to the coming generation the glorious deeds of the Lord, and his might, and the wonders that he has done. (ESV)

Briefly share with the group about a time that you personally experienced the goodness of God. (Consider sharing this story with your children and grandchildren. Even if they already know the story, repeating it will emphasize its importance in their minds.)

**Pray Together**

Close your time together in prayer. Invite some in your group to pray

- for God to strengthen the family ties of each person in the group and to repair any broken relationships;
- for God to calm any anxiety that some may be feeling over what life will be like for them in the empty nest;
- for each person in your group to find a way to rest and to be refreshed.

# Session Four

## Chapters 10-12

**Warm Up**

1. Think back on some of the celebrations you and your family have enjoyed (birthdays, anniversaries, graduations, weddings, retirement, etc.). Tell the group about one or two of your most memorable. What made those particular celebrations special to you?

2. At the end of chapter 10, you were asked to make a list of the positive things you are discovering in the empty nest. Share your list with the group.

**Talk It Over**

3. Why do you think it is important to celebrate achievements and transitions in our lives?

4. Do you think that it would benefit you to celebrate your transition into the empty nest? Why or why not?

5. What hopes do you have for your marriage in the empty nest?

6. At the end of chapter 10 you were asked how you and your friends can spur one another to dream big about your next calling. How did you answer that question?

7. As part of discovering new purpose, Barbara and Susan encouraged us to take inventory of our lives and to try some new things. What five things did they list that we should *know* when trying to learn our new purpose?

8. Share with the group what you are discovering in at least one of the five categories.

9. If you could go back in time and have the opportunity to ask advice from a Take It or Leave It club, what would you ask?

10. Has anyone made an effort to write a personal mission statement? Would you like to share it with the group?

## Take It With You

And I am sure of this, that he who began a good work in you will bring it to completion at the day of Jesus Christ.

Philippians 1:6 ESV

God is always at work in our lives, shaping us to His design and for His purposes. How should this truth affect our hopes, plans, and dreams for what's ahead in the empty nest?

## Pray Together

As you end your study together of the empty nest, pray that each person in your group will

- know the love and nearness of God;
- know the help and pleasure of close friendships;
- experience joy and intimacy in marriage;
- understand her purpose in the next season of life.

# Notes

## Chapter 2: Am I the Only One Who Feels This Way?

1. Anna Quindlen, *Loud and Clear* (New York: Ballantine Books, 2005), 65–67.
2. For more information, visit www.wellspringliving.org.
3. For more information, visit http://onehundredshares.org.

## Chapter 3: What Do I Do With My Loneliness?

1. MOPS stands for Mothers of Preschoolers, an international support network. For more information, visit www.mops.org.

## Chapter 4: What Do I Do With My Disappointments?

1. Paul David Tripp, *Lost in the Middle: Midlife and the Grace of God* (Wapwallopen, PA: Shepherd Press, 2004), 62.
2. Mary Ann Mayo and Joseph Mayo, *The Menopause Manager: A Safe Path for a Natural Change* (Grand Rapids, MI: Baker Books, 2000).
3. F. B. Meyer, *Israel: A Prince With God* (London: Morgan and Scott, n.d.), 16.
4. Larry Crabb, *Shattered Dreams: God's Unexpected Pathway to Joy* (Colorado Springs: WaterBrook, 2002), 4.
5. *The Words of Martin Luther King, Jr.*, ed. Coretta Scott King (New York: New Market Press, 1987), 11.
6. Abby Ellin, "After Full Lives Together, More Older Couples Are Divorcing," *New York Times*, October 30, 2015, http://www.nytimes.com/2015/10/31/your-money/after-full-lives-together-more-older-couples-are-divorcing.html.
7. Xenia P. Montenegro, *The Divorce Experience: A Study of Divorce at Midlife and Beyond*, special report (Washington, D.C.: AARP, May 2004), 4, http://assets.aarp.org/rgcenter/general/divorce.pdf.
8. "New Relationships," DivorceCare small-group curriculum, session 7 (Wake Forest, NC: Church Initiative, 2004), DVD.
9. Tripp, *Lost in the Middle*, 101–102.

## Chapter 5: How Do I Relate to My Husband Now?

1. Oswald Chambers, "My Joy . . . Your Joy," *My Utmost for His Highest*, August 31 (New York: Dodd, Mead & Company, Inc., 1935).
2. For more information, visit www.familylife.com/weekend-to-remember.

## Chapter 6: How Do I Relate to My Adult Kids Now?

1. See http://familylifetoday.com/guest/rosaria-butterfield/ and http://family lifetoday.com/guest/caleb-kaltenbach/. All interviews can be downloaded to your preferred device for listening at your convenience.
2. Glenn Stanton, *The Ring Makes All the Difference: The Hidden Consequences of Cohabitation and the Strong Benefits of Marriage* (Chicago: Moody, 2011), 11–12.
3. See http://familylifetoday.com/guest/glenn-stanton/.
4. Weekend to Remember conferences are presented throughout the U.S. and in many other countries. For information visit www.familylife.com/weekend-to -remember, or call 1-800-FL-TODAY.
5. "Slavery Today," FreeTheSlaves.net, accessed November 16, 2016, http://www .freetheslaves.net/about-slavery/slavery-today/.

## Chapter 7: How Do I Care for My Extended Family?

1. Pew Research Center, *The Sandwich Generation: Rising Financial Burdens for Middle-Aged Americans*, January 30, 2013, page 7, http://www.pewsocialtrends.org /files/2013/01/Sandwich_Generation_Report_FINAL_1-29.pdf.

## Chapter 8: What Do I Do With Me?

1. Robert Robinson, "Come Thou Fount of Every Blessing," 1758.
2. J. I. Packer, *Knowing God's Purpose for Your Life* (Ventura, CA: Regal, 2000), 358.

## Chapter 9: Take a Break!

1. Dan Allender, *To Be Told: Know Your Story, Shape Your Future* (Colorado Springs: WaterBrook, 2005), 3.
2. J. R. R. Tolkien, *The Two Towers*, 2nd ed. (Boston: Houghton Mifflin, 1978), 321.
3. Mrs. Charles E. Cowman, *Springs in the Valley* (Grand Rapids, MI: Zondervan, 1997), 196–197.
4. For more information, visit www.younglife.org.

## Chapter 10: Celebrate!

1. Adapted from the book of Nehemiah.
2. Leviticus 23 describes several of these celebrations. See also Ezra 6; 2 Chronicles 7; Esther 9.
3. These interviews are available at familylifetoday.com/emptynest.

## Chapter 11: Discovering Your New Purpose

1. Sally Kalson, "Brand New 60s for Baby Boomers," *Pittsburgh Post-Gazette*, January 22, 2006, accessed November 2, 2016, www.post-gazette.com/pg/06022/642405-51.stm.

2. Judy Douglass, phone interview, April 2007, and email message to authors, May 3, 2007.

3. Rick and Kay Warren, "Seeing the AIDS Crisis Through God's Eyes," interview by Dennis Rainey and Bob Lepine at the AIDS Summit at Saddleback Church, Lake Forest, California, radio broadcast, *FamilyLife Today*, December 7, 2006, audio file and transcript, http://familylifetoday.com/series/addressing-the-global-aids-crisis/.

4. Ibid.

5. "The Weaver" has been credibly attributed to Florence May Alt (1892), John Banister Tabb (1919), and Grant Colfax Tullar (n.d.), all public domain; a version of the full poem is available at http://www.boltoncthistory.org/granttullar.html.

6. Mary Jenson, *Taking Flight From the Empty Nest: Stories of Fresh Starts When Your Kids Leave Home* (Eugene, OR: Harvest House, 2001), 83.

7. For more information about The Navigators, visit www.navigators.org.

## Chapter 12: Changing Your World

1. Allender, *To Be Told*, 114.

2. Tripp, *Lost in the Middle*, 140.

3. C. T. Studd (1860–1931) was an English missionary who served in India, China, and Africa. Full text of his poem can be found at http://www.cavaliersonly.com/poetry_by_christian_poets_of_the_past/only_one_life_twill_soon_be_past_-_poem_by_ct_studd, accessed November 3, 2016.

4. Colin Welland, *Chariots of Fire*, directed by Hugh Hudson (1981; Warner Brothers); quote said by Eric Liddell as portrayed by Ian Charleson.

**Barbara Rainey** is married to her best friend, Dennis. Their six children are all married, and from five of these six have come twenty-three grandchildren, who call her Mimi. Her favorite name is to be called "friend" by Jesus. Barbara is increasingly in awe at being chosen and loved by Him.

She is also an artist, author, and ambassador, which tell more about what Barbara loves to do. Together Dennis and Barbara started FamilyLife, a ministry of Cru, in 1976. She speaks at Weekend to Remember marriage conferences and is a frequent guest on *Family-Life Today*, a nationally syndicated radio program. She coauthored a number of books with her husband and wrote several herself, including *Thanksgiving: A Time to Remember* and *Letters to My Daughters: The Art of Being a Wife*.

Barbara has begun a new venture within FamilyLife called Ever Thine Home, a holiday and home collection of beautiful and biblical products for women to use to make their homes a witness for their faith.

To learn more about Ever Thine Home and FamilyLife, read the blogs, subscribe to updates, and more, visit them online: everthine home.com and familylife.com.

**Susan Yates** has written fourteen books and speaks both nationally and internationally on the subjects of marriage, parenting, and women's issues. She's the mother of five (including a set of twins), and the grandmother of twenty-one (including a set of quadruplets!). Married for forty-seven years, Susan and her husband, John, live in

Falls Church, Virginia, where John is the senior pastor of The Falls Church Anglican.

But what is she really like? Her blood "bleeds blue." She's a Tarheel, a graduate of the University of North Carolina. She loves Monday Night Football, ACC basketball, shooting hoops with her grandsons, riding horseback with her husband, running, eating chocolate, and talking with girlfriends. You won't find her in the kitchen by choice; she'd rather be outdoors with her golden retriever. Her favorite time of the year is June, when all her kids and grandkids are together for a week of "cousins and family camp" in the foothills of the Shenandoah Mountains of Virginia.

Follow her at www.susanalexanderyates.com.

# More From
# Barbara Rainey

Visit familylifetoday.com for a full list of her books.

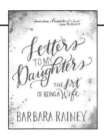

Bestselling author Barbara Rainey understands the challenges newly married couples face. In this insightful book, she offers sage advice on the art of being a wife. Through heartfelt letters, she answers the tough questions and addresses the realities of marriage, sharing personal stories and even mistakes. This is a perfect gift for bridal showers and weddings!

*Letters to My Daughters*

The secret to spiritual growth for couples is more moments together—with each other and with God. Here, the Raineys offer everything couples need to grow in their quiet times together. These short, poignant devotions provide a daily discussion point, prayer, and Scripture reference.

*Moments with You* (with Dennis Rainey)